Waking Up to God

Rediscovering Faith in Post-pandemic Times

— NEIL G. RICHARDSON —

Sacristy
Press

Sacristy Press
PO Box 612, Durham, DH1 9HT

www.sacristy.co.uk

First published in 2022 by Sacristy Press, Durham

Copyright © Neil G. Richardson 2022
The moral rights of the author have been asserted.

All rights reserved, no part of this publication may
be reproduced or transmitted in any form or by
any means, electronic, mechanical photocopying,
documentary, film or in any other format without
prior written permission of the publisher.

Bible extracts, unless otherwise stated, are from the *Revised English Bible*, copyright © Cambridge University Press and Oxford University Press 1989. All rights reserved.

Every reasonable effort has been made to trace the
copyright holders of material reproduced in this
book, but if any have been inadvertently overlooked
the publisher would be glad to hear from them.

Sacristy Limited, registered in England
& Wales, number 7565667

British Library Cataloguing-in-Publication Data
A catalogue record for the book is
available from the British Library

ISBN 978-1-78959-237-5

To Pope Francis

and

*Rowan Williams,
former Archbishop of Canterbury*

Contents

Acknowledgments v
Preface vi
Introduction 1

Chapter 1. Where do we go from here? 14
Chapter 2. The Bible: A book whose time has come? 30
Chapter 3. Jesus: Truly human, truly God? 47
Chapter 4. "Outgrowing God" or Growing into God? 63
Chapter 5. Towards a More Human Church 79
Chapter 6. Joining the Human Race 95
Chapter 7. God and Life 112
Chapter 8. Embracing and Shaping the Future 129

And a Personal Postscript 146
Notes 150

Acknowledgments

I should like to record my thanks to the following people in the writing of this book: Ed Dodman, Donald Eadie, Douglas McIldoon, Steve Phillipson, Tom Stuckey, and my wife and sons, Rhiannon, Mark, James and Simon Richardson.

Preface

This book has been written for a wide range of people. Throughout, I've tried to keep my readers in mind. The range includes young and old, people of different social backgrounds and people of countries and nationalities other than my own. I have in mind, too, people of any faith or no faith. After all, what surely unites us all is our common humanity. To adapt a South African proverb, you're a human being, I'm a human being—so let's start there.

Many people these days are battling with tiredness and anxiety, if not depression and grief as well. The pandemic has taken its toll, and it remains to be seen what its legacy will be. Climate change is a growing worry for us all. The human race has not had to face a challenge like it before. More recently, President Putin's forces have invaded Ukraine, and Europe is a darker place than it has been for several decades.

There are other issues about life itself. What values will we live by as we move into a very uncertain future? What are the things which make for human wellbeing? I'm thinking not just of our families and relationships with each other, but also of what makes for just, happy communities and countries at peace with themselves and each other. Governments, especially democratically elected governments, tend to take short-term views of our future. But progress can't be measured any more just by economic prosperity and election results, important as they are.

And there is, perhaps underlying everything, the question of faith. Is religion something the human race is going to leave behind, as many think or assume? Or might a truly human religion, yet to be discovered and explored—or rediscovered?—take us into a brighter future? In all our crises and the turmoil they generate, where are we to find solid rock for our feet, light for our way, wisdom to live by, hope for the future? It would be presumptuous and arrogant to claim that this book provides these things. But I've attempted at least to ask the questions.

The many people in my mind as I've written this book have included my six grandchildren (ages five to twelve), and their generation. What have they already missed out on, and into what kind of world will they grow up? The generation before them have also missed out—and this in some very serious, far-reaching ways. The younger people are, the less they can be blamed for the state of the planet. But they will be the ones who have to live with it the longest. Many of them are missing out in other ways, too. The housing market in the UK is skewed heavily towards the haves, and many younger people have little or no hope of ever owning their own home. Getting jobs and the rising cost of higher education are two other big worries for them. The education of many has been seriously disrupted by the pandemic.

Against this challenging background, allow me to introduce two particular people who have helped to shape this book. My late father-in-law was a lifelong Christian and Methodist. But he had far more questions than certainties about God. Or so it seemed. When reading his newspaper or hearing the headlines in the media, he would often ask in exasperation, "Why doesn't He (i.e. God) do something about it?" Interestingly, his angry questions didn't prevent him from organizing the annual door-to-door collection for Christian Aid in his village even in his early nineties.

Another person's questions about traditional religion and faith have also shaped this book. Donald introduced himself to me, when I arrived in Leeds as the new minister of the church which he attended or stayed away from, as both a church member and an atheist. He was a distinguished biochemist, quite famous in his later years; in the past, he had been a Methodist lay preacher. Like my father-in-law, he wasn't at all sure how much of traditional Christian faith he accepted. (He may have been adversely affected by a father who was a Methodist minister!) Yet he became, increasingly, an engaging, attractive member of the local church, a warm human being, though hardly an orthodox Christian.

I suspect that there are many people, some still in the churches and lots more outside the churches, with many questions, including those which my grandchildren and their generation will have, not just about faith and God, but about life, human wellbeing and the future of the world.

Much is changing in a crisis-ridden and fast-changing world, including perceptions of what Christian faith really is. That faith isn't what many of us were brought up to think it was. Traditional understandings and interpretations of the Bible have been changing and continue to change. Many people, including myself, are beginning to understand the Bible and Christian faith differently. Yet I believe I remain an orthodox Christian—others will judge! So perhaps a brief word about my background may help.

I spent the first seven years of my life in a blackened, late Victorian terraced house in a road with the splendid name of "Whackhouse Lane". We lived opposite a big textile mill, its tall chimney towering over our house. The loud mill "buzzer" told us, as well as the mill's workforce, the times when work started and finished. Large numbers of that workforce passed our front door four times a day. My parents were or had been millworkers, my mother a weaver, my father still a twister (the process in textile-making before weaving).

I was born ten minutes before my sister. No-one knew beforehand there would be two babies, not one. (Pre-natal knowledge didn't extend that far in those days.)

My father collapsed when told there was another baby on the way. In due course, we were taught to say our prayers at bedtime. Occasionally I added a prayer of my own, like a request to score a goal in my first football match for the school team.

When we were seven, we moved a quarter of a mile away to a council house, as they were then called. We still went to chapel and Sunday School up the hill in Yeadon. Mum and Dad began to attend as well, having spent most Sundays in the 1930s riding a tandem as members of the Headingley Tandem Cycling Club.

At the age of twelve, I made a Christian commitment during an evangelistic campaign at my local church, along with several others about my age. What it all meant at the time I can't now remember. It was, perhaps, a bit of a peer group thing. Two or three years later, a little book called *The Transforming Friendship* helped me a great deal.[1] So did the autobiography of a Christian pop star called Pat Boone. It seemed you could be a Christian and a "normal" teenager after all.

But there was plenty to doubt. A teacher lent me a book called *The Life of Jesus* by a Frenchman called Ernest Renan. It turned out to be a book which was both famous and notorious, depending on your point of view. To my horror, I discovered that Renan didn't believe in the resurrection of Jesus. I speedily returned the book with minimal thanks to my rather amused teacher.

By this time, I had won a scholarship to a prestigious local grammar school whose curriculum was strongly focused on preparing students for the universities of Oxford and Cambridge. So, at the tender age of twelve, I dropped geography and woodwork (failing abysmally in the latter) and took classical Greek instead. (Little good it did me, some years later, trying to order a meal in an Athens restaurant.)

Most of my friends in the sixth form were, in religion, agnostics or atheists. One atheist friend even introduced me to theology. He had discovered *The Shaking of the Foundations* by the theologian Paul Tillich, later well known (and mocked) for calling God "the ground of our being". Soon we were both reading *Honest to God* by John Robinson. This book, written by a bishop of the Church of England, became famous and notorious too. "Our image of God must go," he wrote in an article in *The Observer* announcing the publication of the book in 1963. Both authors challenged traditional language about God. God isn't just "out there" or "up there" ("above the bright blue sky", as one of our Sunday School hymns put it), but beneath us and within us. Robinson predicted that a future age would come to see that he hadn't been radical enough. In a final newspaper article, written when he knew he was dying of cancer, he expressed his conviction that "God is to be found in the cancer as in everything else".[2]

John Robinson popularized the idea that doubting and questioning were as much part of Christian faith as conviction and certainty. My college chaplain at university encouraged me to think of being a Christian as "living with questions".

University life involved me in student politics. I was nearly sent down for leading a food boycott at my college. I survived, because my history tutor persuaded the senior common room by his argument that "Richardson doesn't look like a revolutionary to me".

After two varied, eye-opening years teaching, first in Sierra Leone and then in inner-city Birmingham, I trained to be a Methodist minister, spending much of my later ministry teaching the Bible, mainly the New Testament. In the early years, fundamentalist students gave me a difficult time. (I discount the occasion when, in a Greek class, one responded to my enquiry, "I take it everyone knows what a preposition is ... ", with the reply, "Isn't that when a woman comes up to you and makes a naughty suggestion?")

Most important of all, I married Rhiannon in the year before going to Oxford as a full-time church minister, hospital chaplain and student chaplain. (Churches like to keep their ministers busy.) Early on in my ministry I had to face the question: which vows were more important—my marriage vows or my ordination vows? The question relates closely to a major theme of this book: does religion make us more or less human?

I wrote most of this book during the UK's first lockdown, due to Covid-19. For my wife Rhiannon and myself, now retired and living on the borders of Shropshire and Herefordshire, those weeks were not an unpleasant time. Unlike so many people in that crisis, we didn't have to worry about earning our living, and we could walk from our front door up country lanes. Naturally, we worried for our families, each couple struggling to sustain their own careers whilst home-schooling their children. But it was already becoming clear that the suffering, loss and disruption caused by Covid were confronting not just individuals, but communities, churches and whole countries, with new problems and challenges. There is hardly a country in the world which has escaped the pandemic, and none that can hide from a changing climate.

Covid-19 news dominated newspapers, radio and television for two years and more. What was going on in Africa or the Middle East we hardly heard about. Now, other pressing issues are beginning to dominate our front pages again. The repercussions of the Russian invasion of Ukraine will be long-lasting. The UK will continue to adjust, painfully or otherwise, to life outside the European Union. The crisis of climate change becomes more urgent with every year that passes.

So this is part of the background—personal, national and international—to this book. One of its themes is, quite simply, our common humanity, and where we should be going. Like many ordained ministers of the Church, in the course of my work I was often greeted by the remark, "I'm not religious ... ". I never really worked out what my response should be. But the remark of an Anglican Franciscan monk many years ago has been a guiding light for me: "It's more important to be human than religious." The Church is nothing if not more human than religious. Which brings me to marathon-running.

Long-distance running has been a favourite recreation ever since school and university. Running the London Marathon in 2004 was a seminal moment for me. (I remain, I think, the only national church leader who ran it whilst in office.) It set me thinking about what joining the human race means in practice. It's very easy for us all to be semi-detached, rather than fully engaged members. We human beings are the most question-begging species on the planet. What are we? What are we supposed to be?

We share the planet with countless other creatures, so this introduction might be a good place to make brief reference to our (departed) two Golden Retrievers. The philosophy of Tess (1975–85) seemed to be: if something moves, chase it; if it doesn't, try eating it. Simba (1987–95), by contrast, appeared to have an identity crisis: was he male or female? Many male dogs thought he was female, and some became quite aggressive when they found he wasn't. Generally speaking, however, whatever their personal idiosyncrasies, dogs, cats and most other creatures I can think of are relatively easy to define. In contrast, the range of behaviour and character, aims and lifestyles of human beings is enormous.

So this book is written on the premiss that three pressingly urgent questions of today are inter-related.

There is the human question: who or what are we, and how do we fulfil our true potential (whatever that is)? There is the closely related question of our common future, and, especially now, the future of the earth we share. And, thirdly, there is the question of a god or a creator: is there such a reality?

Earlier, I mentioned Donald, the biochemist and member of my church who introduced himself to me as an atheist. I have since met other churchgoers who consider themselves atheists. But the concept of atheism, as Rowan Williams points out, may be a less simple idea than many people assume: "If we want to understand what atheism means, we need to know which gods are being rejected and why."[3]

This is a book which changed direction in the course of the Covid-19 pandemic. In the autumn of 2019, I came across Richard Dawkins' latest book *Outgrowing God*. Perhaps many readers of this book will have read, or heard of, Dawkins' best-seller *The God Delusion*. His name will occur from time to time in these pages. Three things about him are perhaps worth stating briefly.

First, he is a brilliant writer and particularly a brilliant polemicist who has rendered the Christian faith and Church a valuable service by challenging concepts and views of God which are untenable—views which all Christians should have rejected years ago. Second, his attack has been confined almost entirely to fundamentalist Christianity. As far as I know, he rarely engages with more mainstream forms of Christianity.

Thirdly, he does not seem to have taken the trouble to inform himself properly and thoroughly about the things he is attacking—particularly the Bible and those mainstream understandings of God and creation. But he has helped me see more clearly both the human and the faith questions which urgently need to be addressed. Out of this reading, my own experience and, most of all, current crises come the three questions which provide the material for this book.

Introduction

Three big questions

We begin by looking more closely at our three big questions: our common future—now so problematical and uncertain; ourselves, the unpredictable species anthropologists have called *homo sapiens*; and, thirdly, the question of God: is God as obsolete as Richard Dawkins and other scientists seem to think?

Our future: Where are we heading?

Bill Bryson's book, *A Short History of Nearly Everything*, is a brilliant survey of the history of the universe, our planet, and the emergence of human life. The last, short section is called "The Road to Us". The final paragraphs highlight the challenges of the future. He concludes:

> If this book has a lesson, it is that we are awfully lucky to be here—and by 'we' I mean every living thing. To attain any kind of life in this universe appears to be quite an achievement....

> We have arrived at this position of eminence in a stunningly short time. Behaviourally modern human beings have been around for no more than about 0.0001 per cent of Earth's history—almost nothing, really....

And his final paragraph:

> We really are at the beginning of it all. The trick, of course, is to make sure we never find the end. And that, almost certainly, will require a lot more than lucky breaks.[4]

Many people think that history is speeding up. The rate of change seems to be increasing. Or is that the delusion of a 70+ like me? Whether so or not, we seem to be coming to a point in history where we humans are globally more aware of each other than we have ever been. Until the eighteenth century, the rest of the world was unaware of the existence of Australia and New Zealand, not to mention many Pacific Islands. In the nineteenth century, means of communication were becoming easier and faster, but nothing like what they have become.

At the same time as all these changes have been occurring, our perspective on time has been revolutionized. In the Christian world, if not elsewhere, most people believed until well into the nineteenth century that God created the world not only in seven days, but, even more precisely, in 4004 BC. In the light of our new perspective, formed by Darwin's theory of evolution, fossil discoveries and much more, we have, I hope, now firmly rejected that timescale.

It puts the Bible's time references in a quite different light. I'll return to this, but let's note for now two fundamental changes. Our new understanding of how old the universe and the planet are, and the millennia preceding our evolution, has given biblical phrases like "in the last days" (Acts 2:17) and "this the final age" (Hebrews 1:2) a new perspective and significance.[5]

The second major change is how we now view the Bible's "take" on the future. For centuries some Christians have been predicting that "the end is nigh". It still may be—at least for us humans. But some scholars are now suggesting that we have taken too literally some of the Bible's "end of the world" language. And did the first Christians, like Paul, expect the end of the world in their lifetimes? So many have thought. But, again, we may have read too much into their words.

So we shall be asking pressing questions about our common future. What kind of creatures have we humans been designed (programmed?) to be? And if there is a Creator behind it all, into what kind of future is he (or she) calling us?[6]

The question of ourselves: What are we, and what are we to make of ourselves?

The three questions which have shaped this book are connected. The question of the future is, in large part, the question of *homo sapiens*: what are we and what are we supposed to be? Can we go on as we are? Very briefly, during the first lockdown of the pandemic, some of us glimpsed a world in which much of the traffic—road, air and sea—had greatly diminished. It has since started up again, but maybe the brief experience of a quieter, less hectic world imprinted on our minds the poet's observation:

> The world is too much with us; late and soon,
> Getting and spending we lay waste our powers.

The poet was William Wordsworth. He may have had a point, but we can't earn a living from looking at daffodils. Even so, *homo sapiens* has become, in the last 150 years or so, *homo oeconomos*. And that is a one-dimensional view of what we are and what we might be.

Somehow we have acquired what someone once described as "a container" view of time—i.e. pack as much into each day as you possibly can. In fact, many of us incline to measure the success or otherwise of each day by how much we have done.

Ordained ministers like myself can end up trying to justify ourselves. ("See how busy I am!") I began my ministry as if I was running a hundred-yard sprint. After two months, I was exhausted. Fortunately, the phone rang, and a monk I had met two years before asked if he could come to stay. I began to learn that our lives can't be measured just by how much we pack into them. Whether that phone call was coincidence or providential is an interesting question. William Temple, a great but all too short-lived Archbishop of Canterbury, once suggested: "When I stop praying, coincidences stop happening."

My early experience illustrates the problem which more and more people face: can we, should we, continue to live as frenetically as we have been? Can we go on traversing the globe in the way we have been? Almost certainly not. Can we go on accumulating things, including experiences, and places we have been and people we have met? We might ask: why should we? Do they really add to our human happiness and wellbeing?

The advice of the twelfth-century Cistercian abbot and reformer Bernard of Clairvaux becomes important: give yourself/selves some attention. We easily take ourselves for granted, simply getting on with life. Or we put important personal issues to the back of our minds, especially if we're busy. Bernard had a point: give yourself some attention! That's not a call to self-indulgence or selfishness, but an invitation to face life's most fundamental questions. What, really, are we—and who am I? What are we for? What is the best way to live? What should my priorities and deepest values really be?

What is the Bible's "take" on human beings? Many think that its first and last word about us all is that we are sinners. But that's quite mistaken. The Bible has a surprisingly high view of us, expressed in its first chapter (Genesis 1:27): made in the image of God.

Other parts of the Bible say similar things. A psalm echoes this—or it might be the writer of Genesis echoing the writer of the psalm: "What is ... a human being ... ? You have made him little less than a god" (Psalm 8:4–5).

Surely, we suspect, St Paul takes a dim view of human beings and human nature? (St Paul wouldn't be our first choice to keep us company on a desert island.) But we would be largely wrong. One of the root meanings of the biblical word "sin" is "missing the mark"—falling short of the target, as in archery practice. "The target" in this case is the glory of God (Romans 3:23), which might be defined, not as some heavenly existence with or without harps, but as "human beings at their best".

The modern discovery of two largely lost Christian writers from earlier centuries, Mother Julian of Norwich, author of *Revelations of Divine Love*, and the seventeenth-century poet, priest and theologian Thomas Traherne, has helped especially in the rediscovery of lost emphases of the Christian faith. Mother Julian's use of the image of a mother, applied both to God and to Jesus, has challenged our old patriarchal language. Traherne's emphasis on the enjoyment of the world is a greatly under-played theme, too. (I return to this in Chapter 7.)

An Anglican parish priest startled his congregation many years ago by putting a large notice on the noticeboard outside the church: "This church is for sinners only." Regular worshippers stopped attending, and said they wouldn't return until the notice was taken down.

But their priest had a point. Christians, so far from claiming to be morally superior to others, are supposed to be among the first to confess they are sinners (i.e. falling short of our potential as human beings).

God and the danger of losing God

Our three questions are connected. For example, the word "hypocrite" appears frequently in the Gospels. Originally meaning "actor", in the New Testament it comes to mean keeping up appearances, being judgemental towards others, pretending to be what we are not—all these things. What is crucial is this: if our view of our God is skewed, how we see our fellow-human beings will be skewed too. If we think of God as judgemental, we shall view other people in the same way.

Questions about God are amongst the most fundamental—perhaps *the* most fundamental—questions our world faces. Is God real? Is God and our relationship to God fundamental to the wellbeing of the world? If there is a Creator, it is reasonable to suggest that the Creator might indeed be key to the health both of ourselves and the planet. It is a pity that a proverb, quoted many times in the Bible, has been so misunderstood: "The fear of the Lord is the beginning of wisdom" (Proverbs 9:10, cf. 1:7). The Revised English Bible translated this as: "The first step to wisdom is the fear of the Lord."

There is a "double whammy" here. First, "fear" suggests "being afraid of"—a natural enough response, perhaps, to a transcendent Mystery we call God. Yet "fear" here means "recognizing the reality of", "awe", "wonder".

The second problem word is "wisdom". Does our modern world know what this is? It doesn't appear, so far as I know, in school curricula. Yet most religious traditions of the world over many centuries have sought it, prized it, regarded it as "the pearl of great price". The Bible teaches that wisdom, whatever it is, was and always has been fundamental in the design of creation.

Most of us in the so-called "developed" world respond in one of three different ways to the question of God. Either God doesn't exist—end of story. Or, God is irrelevant, so just get on with your life. Or, God probably exists ("I believe in a God"—whatever that means), but, like people who only think about politics at election time or in a crisis, we can forget about God most of the time. So even if God exists, God tends to be a mysterious, marginal reality whose relevance to the world is far from clear.

This goes for many people who attend church as well as for those who don't. Either way, through unexamined belief in God or outright disbelief, I suggest that we are "losing" God. I take a risk here in using the word "lose". I don't mean to imply that God is a sort of cosmic Cheshire Cat whose outline in and over the world gradually fades away as fewer and fewer people believe in him. If God is utterly real, as I believe, we can't really lose God at all. But to say that could make us dangerously complacent or optimistic in multiple crises where there are no grounds for either complacency or optimism (hope—real hope—is a different matter). And is it possible that losing God might put us at risk of losing ourselves?

Many of us today take God for granted, marginalize God or don't believe in God at all. That surely goes without saying. But do we understand what we are rejecting? Real belief in the real God has practical outcomes—and so has not believing in God. Atheism has outcomes too. So does practical atheism, and there is a lot of that about. Practical atheism might be defined as paying lip service to the existence of God but living our lives as if God doesn't exist. Either way, there can be, and are, consequences. National and international life across the world bears this out. If we really believed in the reality of a Creator, would the arms race be the monstrous evil it is? Would refugees be pushed from pillar to post? Would the gap between rich and poor be as grotesque as it is? We organize ourselves most of the time as if there were no God.

I'll come in a moment to the consequences of this loss of God. In my view, they are already proving serious and far-reaching. But first I need to acknowledge that older ways of thinking about God don't help. They have fostered the idea that God is detached and remote from life—perhaps there for us in an emergency, but that's all. Most of the time, life simply goes on. Yet there is the closest possible connection between God and life, between God and the universe. Shouldn't that be obvious—especially if God is the Creator of both life and the universe? Perhaps. But older readers may recall being told in their childhood that God is in a place called "heaven". And if we wondered where that was, an old Sunday School hymn told us: "above the bright blue sky."

Ideas about prayer—and often our experience of praying—can strengthen the notion of a God who is detached and disconnected from life. In our prayers we have tended to ask God to *intervene*. If the prayer was answered, it "proved" God had done so. But there have always been apparently "unanswered" prayers, so maybe we are missing something here about the nature of both prayer and God.

I shall have much to say later about prayer. But these traditional ways of thinking about God are misleading. For example, people who "intervene" are people who weren't involved in the situation in the first place. But if God is real, and if God is, as the Bible and Christian faith claim, the world's Creator, then God is anything but marginal to life and the world. God is at the heart of both, and so utterly vital to our future and even our survival. In the eighteenth century, there was a popular idea of God the Creator as a kind of celestial watchmaker who designed the world, "wound it up", and left it to tick, whilst he retired to heaven. I caricature a little, but the prevalence of the model lingers on in the subconscious, and writers like Richard Dawkins appear to think that it's the only "model" of God on offer. It's not difficult to see how irrelevant and marginal such a retired inventor would be—unless, of course, he *intervenes*. And if we regard "miracles" as a rough guide to the number of divine interventions, that would appear to be not very often.

But suppose God actually *pervades* the whole of life—indeed the entire universe? Suppose such a reality is closer to us even than our own breathing? This is the reality to which the Bible points—*pace* Richard Dawkins' crude caricatures of the God of the Bible.

Central to the argument of this book is that the questions of who we are and who or what God is are integrally connected. It is possible that we and our Creator are *relational* in nature. If that is so, no wonder the loss of God is so serious. It entails the loss of ourselves.

A summary and a question: A downward spiral?

In an earlier book, I sketched a downward spiral outlined by Paul in his letter to the Romans.[7] The first step on the downward slope is when we take God and life for granted, or centre our lives on substitute gods. Taking life for granted implies taking for granted the Creator who gave us life. Substitute gods, as I hope to show in the next chapter, make us less than human. Richard Dawkins seems to think that he has explained us human beings by tracing our evolutionary development. But he hasn't. He has highlighted a wonderful mystery: here we are, but what a question-begging species we are! What will we make of ourselves?

But taking God and life for granted impoverishes us. We may be unaware of our impoverishment much of the time, but it starts to show—especially in the way we take other people for granted, or, worse still, ignore them when they need us. Communities start to fall apart, relationships fray, beautiful things like sex are cheapened—the downward spiral goes on. This is St Paul's second step on the downward spiral. In his language, human minds are "darkened", and we are dehumanized.

Earlier centuries thought of God as the *ens realissimum*. The Latin here is almost recognizable: God is the most real reality there is—fundamental to everything—behind, beneath, in it all.

So what are we doing to ourselves and the planet when we cease to believe, in any down-to-earth practical sense, in the real God?

I hope this Introduction has helped to show how interrelated our three questions are. If we are to create and embrace a future which is human and happy, we need to attend to who we are and what we are meant to be, and to attend to our Creator.

CHAPTER 1

Where do we go from here?

Side-stepping questions is developing into an art form. Many of us can see or hear it practised most days on the radio or television. Social media also present their own challenges to anyone intent on discovering the truth. Big questions are particularly awkward—questions which we avoid or forget about most of the time. This book has begun to address three:

- what are we human beings; what are we for, and how do we function best?
- who or what is God, if there is a god, and what difference, if any, does that make?
- what does the future hold, and can we choose and shape it?

The question of the future now seems the most urgent. But our common future may depend a great deal on our answers to the first two: the questions about ourselves and God. That determines the order of this chapter.

What are we and how do we function best?

I referred in the Introduction to the predictability of creatures other than humans—with occasional exceptions like Simba, our second Golden Retriever. Who would have thought he would be found, early one morning, "queueing" for cheese (of which he was very fond) outside the local delicatessen? He was, shall we say, a little eccentric. But, Simba's apart, the behaviour of animals is at least more predictable than human behaviour tends to be. We are a question-begging species. Bill Bryson's book, quoted in the Introduction, puts it in evolutionary perspective very well:

> If you were designing an organism to look after life in our lonely cosmos, to monitor where it is going and keep a record of where it has been, you wouldn't choose human beings for the job .... But ... we have been chosen, by fate or providence or whatever you choose to call it. As far as we can tell, we are the best there is. It's an unnerving thought that we may be the living universe's supreme achievement and its worst nightmare simultaneously.[8]

I am writing in the immediate aftermath of the Covid pandemic. It has made still clearer crucial questions about ourselves—the human race—which have been looming ever larger at this stage in our history. What sort of creatures are we? What is our potential? Is it possible to say what we are meant to be, or, at least, what makes for human flourishing?

It's easy to take ourselves for granted and to forget these deeper questions. There are more immediate challenges and opportunities: earning a living, bringing up a family, making the most of life .... There are wider challenges as well, such as managing national economies, negotiating international relations, and, now more pressing than ever, looking after the planet.

But the deeper questions won't go away. There have recently been good stories to tell about us human beings. During the pandemic, neighbourliness and compassion were plentiful. There has been no shortage of volunteers. Medical staff and care workers have risked their health and even their lives.

But there has been a darker side. The pandemic crowded out of our news bulletins and our newspapers what is happening in other countries. "Britain first", "America first" etc. may seem a natural response for a country to make, especially in a crisis. But it's hardly compassionate, or even wise. As many have said, Covid is the responsibility of us all. To act as if one country can solve its problems in isolation, ignoring the rest, is foolish, as well as selfish. The pandemic exposed both what we can be at our best and what we may be at our worst.

A fault line seems to run through us human beings. Other creatures are relatively easy to define. The range of behaviours and character, aims and lifestyles of human beings is enormous. The fault line is apparent almost from our earliest days. At our worst, we can emulate "nature red in tooth and claw". At our best—perhaps it's not yet clear what our best might be. The ancient Greeks advised "Know yourself". A monk I once knew suggested that self-knowledge comprised three-fifths of Christianity.

In previous centuries questions other than living standards and national economies received a lot of attention. (There wasn't much they could do about living standards.) In the Introduction I referred briefly to a concept increasingly alien, it seems, in our contemporary, technological cultures: wisdom. What is wisdom—the secret of life, and the best way to live it? Where is wisdom to be found? A down-to-earth example—to which I return later in the book—is our attitude to time. We tend to measure the success of each day by how much we've done or earned.

So what are we? The creation of artificial intelligence (robots) sharpens the question. Some scientists have a bleakly reductionist view of humans. For example, "We are physical beings made of large collections of particles governed by nature's laws. Everything we do and everything we think amounts to motions of those particles."[9] Even our consciousness, the author contends, will ultimately be explicable in this way. More probable, I suggest, is the argument that "consciousness cannot be satisfactorily reduced to physics *without subtracting something*".[10] The same author points out that thinking is what humans do, computers never will.[11]

Yet the advent of labour-saving robots may pose the question: what is life for? If most of us won't have to work for our living, what are we all going to do? Labour-saving devices and mass-production of all kinds of things have been, for decades now, bringing questions like these ever nearer. Now they loom larger than ever. Will we, before long, work only because, otherwise, we shall be bored? Yet, even here, AI (robots doing human work?) is already depriving people of jobs they used to have. Hopefully, more of us will be able to work in more creative ways, so that work and leisure don't need to be distinguished quite as sharply as they have been.

Questions about human communities loom large too. Is there an optimum size for a city? Is a liberal democracy the best way to govern ourselves? How much equality should there be? Do we need a much stronger "united nations"? The questions multiply.

The Covid-19 crisis brought to the fore remarkable human qualities—self-sacrifice for others, helping vulnerable neighbours and much more. Will it all survive the present crisis? How can we build on the good? Instead of just keeping ourselves busy, instead of only, or mainly, trying to grow our economies, outdo other countries, and improve our living standards year on year, there are deeper questions to face. But that may mean also facing the question of God—or, at least, whether there is a god at all.

Who or what is "God"? And does it make any difference?

Our eldest son, at the age of two, surprised us once by suddenly announcing that God had come down from heaven. "And then", he added, "God went to Norway." (His revered grandfather was a geologist who went every summer to do research in Norway.) Our eldest grandson, on first going to church and seeing the minister, asked in an awed whisper, "Is that God?"

At home, school, church and elsewhere, millions of children pick up immature, garbled and sometimes quite wrong understandings of God. To very many people, the word "god" is primarily a swear word. The Bible, understood literally, may make the situation worse. We've all a lot of "God stuff" to work through—if we ever do. Many think science has disproved God anyway. Many have concluded that God—whoever or whatever—is irrelevant to life, though perhaps worth a try with a quick prayer in an emergency.

So is God real? That's a better way of putting the question than asking if God exists. I've no intention of trying to prove what can't be proved—whether God is real or not. But it's important, I think, to point out how mistaken and even confused some eminent scientists have been and still are on this subject.

Richard Dawkins rightly assumes, to judge from the title of his latest book, *Outgrowing God*, that there is some growing up to be done. But he appears not to have considered the possibility of *growing into* a more mature understanding of God. Many people have pointed out that the god Dawkins rejects doesn't correspond with the God of Christian faith at all.

More particularly, Dawkins appears not to understand the Christian doctrine of creation. If he did, he would know there is no competition between that belief and evolution. Christians believe that God made the world out of nothing. That can't be explained, proved or even investigated (as if it could be) scientifically. Creation out of nothing is more like the work of a writer or composer. So anyone who says "There is no god"—as anyone is entitled to do—should at least ask themselves what it is they are denying. "God" is certainly not a kind of supernatural being, one stage further back than "the Big Bang", tinkering with atoms etc. Many people have left behind the view of God they picked up at junior church or in school assemblies thinking it was "the real thing", when it was probably nothing of the kind. The question of God, anyway, is one we tend to avoid; it's awkward, disturbing—even threatening. Like politics in the pulpit in the view of some churchgoers: better to keep the lid on what looks like a hornets' nest. But if we adopt such avoidance tactics, what are we depriving ourselves of?

Of course, many people have good reason for not believing in God. They are revolted by the cruelty of the world, by nature (sometimes) "red in tooth and claw", or by God's apparent absence when a prayer was not answered as they had desperately hoped. Most religions of the world have wrestled with the problems of suffering and of evil, and it will be vital to return to this. There are no simple or easy answers, even if many people, religious and otherwise, sometimes give the impression there are. How a person responds to suffering, whether their own or the world's, is crucial. I shall want to suggest that it's the acid test of any faith worth having.

To many, "God" may seem to be a mysterious reality whose relevance to the world is far from clear when we have to live in "the real world". But suppose God is utterly *essential* to the world—woven into it, as it were—so much so, that the only real world is, in fact, one with the Creator at its centre? What if the real God—if there is one—is very different from what we supposed?

In just three places, the Bible comes close to "defining" God—who (by definition!) is indefinable: God is "spirit" (or "breath"—the original Hebrew and Greek mean both); God is "light"; and God is "love". These "definitions", whether true or not, take us a long way from traditional ideas of a god "up there" or "out there"—a long way, even, from God as a supernatural being.

First, by these definitions, God is the spirit or power which "breathes" life into the world. It's as if (a distinguished historian once wrote), if God stopped breathing, the universe would cease to exist. Second, God is "light"—that is, the truth or reality which shines through everything, including ourselves. And third, God is love—the definition most quoted and misunderstood of the three, not least by Christians. It is not the same as saying *either* "there is a supernatural being who loves" *or* "Love is God". In the latter case, human love would determine who God is, whereas the Bible says God's love is like, but even greater than, human love at its best.

So if God is the spirit or breath, light and love at the very heart of the universe, then such a God (always supposing God is real) will be essential not only to our existence, but also to our deepest wellbeing and happiness. Our own experience sometimes seems to point that way. When a child is not loved enough, she will be insecure, unhappy or even worse. Parents may be blamed, but maybe they weren't loved either. Similarly, light and transparency are important; propaganda is dangerous, and fake news toxic.

The question of "God" is difficult to separate from the question of what we are. In the Introduction I suggested that we and our Creator, if real, are *relational*. Does that mean that, in some sense, we are "spiritual" beings? The word "spiritual" can be misleading, especially if contrasted with words like "material" or "physical". But we are beginning to see in these crises that human beings need more than just bread. How do we keep well and healthy minds and hearts—in the sense of our innermost beings? It need not surprise us that more people practise disciplines like meditation and mindfulness.

So what are we doing to ourselves and the planet when we cease to believe, in any down-to-earth practical sense—in spirit, truth and love—what the Bible "defines" as "God"? Ordinary human words are not exact or "big" enough to describe this mystery. Religious traditions, including Christianity, have taught that it's easier to say what God is not than what God is. This idea has, down the centuries, been fundamental to the Christian tradition, known as "*apophatic*" (from the Greek word meaning "negative").

Older ways of thinking about God don't always help. Our prayers asking God to "intervene" can strengthen the notion of a God disconnected from life. Some people ask: did God send the pandemic? That can't be so if God is compassionate and loving. So what of stories in the Bible which seem to say that God *does* send plagues etc.?

In response, it's important to notice: *the Bible has no concept of secondary causation.* That is, biblical writers thought of God as directly causing everything. But we can't now take literally that biblical picture of God. Daniel Defoe's account of the Great Plague of 1665 provides interesting contrasts and similarities with contemporary responses to Covid, not least in the role of Providence. In this respect, Defoe is much closer to the biblical world than we are. I believe that we now may not grudgingly admit, but gladly recognize, that God doesn't "control" the world in the way we used to think. God doesn't micro-manage the universe. For better or worse, our Creator seems to have given us more "leeway". But that need not mean God does nothing. Later chapters will explore this crucial claim.

The question of suffering will also have to be addressed. Even if God didn't send the coronavirus, a supposedly almighty God must have allowed it.[12]

And what of our personal lives? Can we still believe that our Creator has "a plan" for each of us? I believe we can—not in the sense that God has got everything mapped out for us. That can't be true if we have a measure of free will. But Christian faith continues to teach that God is personal. In a world as impersonal as ours seems to be, can that belief still be sustained?

Finding our future

To summarize thus far, I'm suggesting that our future depends a great deal on our facing up to fundamental questions about ourselves and about God. At the time of writing, the future looks daunting. The world is emerging—just—from the throes of a pandemic. But its dire effects will be with us for a long time: national economies battered, international co-operation severely stretched, and an imminent threat of widespread hunger. So the question of our common future is a pressing one. Not surprisingly, political leaders talk about "progress" less than they used to. International diplomacy and action are beginning to look more and more like firefighting. Crises seem to multiply, and looming over them all is the threat posed by climate change and the galloping deterioration of our environment.

The future is far from being a blank sheet on which we write what we want. "Freedom of choice" is a beguiling but deeply misleading mantra. How free are we, given the fault line which seems to run through the human race? To ask this question is not to be pessimistic either about the future or about ourselves. Being realistic and finding the secret of hope, I suggest, offers a better way forward.

A fourth definition in the Bible is important to our argument:

> This is the judgement: the light has come into the world, but people preferred darkness to light because their deeds were evil (John 3:19).

For example, a nation may prefer its illusions: it is "exceptional", and should be "first". There's always something which makes "my country" special and specially deserving. A nation tends to choose its memories—even distort them. The statues it erects can be revealing. Most nations, and especially those with an imperial past, have memories which they might want to forget, and others which, however valued, may need correcting.

As with the importance of love in human life, psychologists and counsellors advise: come to terms with the past; don't bury it. Our human preference for "darkness" rather than light, for illusion and propaganda rather than truth, runs deep and wide. As the poet T.

S. Eliot observed, "humankind cannot bear very much reality". The original Greek word for judgement in the verse quoted earlier from John's Gospel is *krisis*, meaning not only "judgement", but also "turning-point": faced with the choice of facing light, truth and reality, or hiding from them.

What kind of future are we creating—or sleepwalking into? To focus on our three leading "god" terms, if we can't "breathe", because (the) "spirit" has been squeezed out, if we can't "see" because we can no longer distinguish truth from propaganda and fake news, and if we neglect to encourage and nurture love amongst ourselves, are we not in danger of sliding into a suffocating, darkened, loveless world in which spiritual and moral capital begin to seep away?

This loss of God easily goes by default. But I've suggested that taking God for granted (in the sense in which I've defined "god") may easily slide into taking life and other people for granted. Worse still, we might ignore each other, look the other way, for example, rather than acknowledge the humanity of the homeless person on the pavement at our feet. If, like my own country, we have spent half a century not even sure there is such a thing as "society", no wonder communities begin to fall apart, relationships fray, and beautiful things like sex are cheapened. There is a downward spiral and the loss of "air" to breathe, light to see by and love to keep us warm is the first step.[13]

In my own country, "freedom of choice" has been an article of faith, a mantra since at least 1979, when Mrs Thatcher came to power. But some people have more choice than others. The poorest have very little choice indeed. If rich, successful people think otherwise, it may be because they rarely or never encounter struggling human beings; their way of life insulates them from such unsettling encounters. As we shall see in the next chapter, Adam, the first human being of the biblical myth, wasn't free to choose, despite what many have thought.

Many people today think history is accelerating. Change occurs at an ever-faster rate—new technologies, new achievements, and greater capability for good or evil. We have also reached a point in history where we are globally more aware of each other than we have ever been. News and information of all kinds travel faster and further than ever. Our reach goes on extending: how much space travel might there be in years to come? And the climate is changing—with all the challenges and dangers that creates.

Happiness is surely a desirable goal. Human beings can agree about that. But happiness can be elusive. Can a person be selfish and happy? No doubt they can—up to a point. But what about everyone else? And can such a person self-isolate indefinitely? The lure of nostalgia and the attraction of "escape to the country" are not panaceas for the challenges we face.

With the goal of peace, similar questions apply. Can one country enjoy peace if it self-isolates? Hardly—not in today's and tomorrow's world. A country seeking happiness in self-isolation would have to build walls, for example, to repel all refugees and other migrants. Could it be economically self-sufficient anyway? And what if other countries kept intruding on that country's isolationism? And what of the world itself? With the climate changing so drastically and alarmingly, there is, increasingly, nowhere to hide.

The question of justice—for everyone—looms large in the question of our common future. Justice demands a far greater measure of equality amongst us. All human lives matter. But we tend to behave as if some lives matter far more than others.

The question of the future is, in large part, the question of *homo sapiens*: what are we and what are we supposed to be? And that, I suggest, raises not just economic questions, but moral and spiritual ones, too. The question of "God"—or, at the very least, questions about the spirit, light and love vital to our wellbeing—can hardly be avoided.

In the past, Christians have talked much about a future "salvation", with the focus on the individual, and how the individual might escape hell and get to heaven. But the Bible's perspective is wider than this. The Hebrew word for salvation, *shalom*, denotes our (as well as "my") deepest wellbeing in this life. The New Testament enriches, widens and deepens this understanding of human wellbeing. Christians believe in life before death as well as life after death (on this, see especially Chapter 4). The Bible also has much to say about the wellbeing of the earth and creation. In fact, almost from start to finish, the Bible has a future focus.

I observed earlier that the question "Where is wisdom to be found?" has been a leading one in human communities and especially religious traditions for much of our recorded history. It has become marginalized only in modern times. But perhaps it provides the vital connection which binds together the three questions we have been exploring in this chapter. If we are to create and embrace a future which is human and happy, we need to attend to who we are and what we are meant to be. But the question of "God" may well be the most important of the three. If "God" is as essential as the very breath, light and love (or heart) necessary to our survival and wellbeing, then our common future as humans depends on our response to that mystery.

CHAPTER 2

The Bible: A book whose time has come?

People can get upset when their long-held views about the Bible are challenged. A man mournfully said to me once: "Christmas will never be the same again." Yet how can we hang on to views of the Bible which scientists and scholars have shown to be wrong? The Bible can't be six feet above contradiction, as preachers are often (wrongly) supposed to be. What is more, in a globalized world we have begun to discover how much the great religions of the world have in common. I'll say more about this when we discuss the person of Jesus in the coming chapter.

So the Bible's authority can't be simply assumed. Churchgoers and non-churchgoers alike need to be more open with their criticisms of the Bible: "a horrible story", "impossible teaching", and so on. In any case, if the Bible provides important clues to the mystery of "God", then that "God" can handle such criticisms. The God of the Bible, *pace* Richard Dawkins and his fellow "new atheists", isn't a violent, jealous patriarch. These views derive from a fundamentalist, selective reading of the Bible. Nor was the Bible ever meant, again *pace* Dawkins, to be a history book. Its writers aren't infallible. For example, St Luke gets a few facts wrong, and St Paul can be sarcastic, even pastorally inept.

Classics—such as Shakespeare's plays, and especially religious classics like the Bible—have a way of generating a new following and new interpretations in century after century. So now, current events are throwing new light on old texts, illuminating them with new significance and relevance. Perhaps it's time to look at the Bible with fresh eyes. To start here need not contradict a more familiar starting-point for many Christians: the authority of the Bible as "the word of God". I commend a practical definition of "authority": "a (or *the*?) source of life, truth and growth".

In this chapter, we focus first on creation and the Creator; second, on God and gods—a fundamental distinction in the Bible; and third, on the Bible's distinctive "take" on the end of the world. A short conclusion will link this chapter with the previous one and its focus on our key questions about ourselves, "God" and our future.

The Creator's gamble

The promises of God run through the Bible like a golden thread. Beginning with Israel and spreading in the New Testament to the whole human race, God promises life, land and wellbeing ("salvation"). First of all, however, comes God's promise to Noah after the Flood.

The story of the Flood is one of the best known in the whole Bible. My children had a jigsaw based on it; my grandchildren have it in lavishly illustrated story books. But no-one, I hope, believes it. It tells the story of how the Creator God ran out of patience with his still-new world, drowning everyone and everything in unrelenting rain. Only Noah and his family escaped in the ark, together with two animals of each species, as God had instructed. After the earth dried out, God started all over again.

The story may be an ancient memory of a flood long ago. But that isn't the point. We mustn't throw out the baby with the floodwater. At the end of the story, God says, "Never again". But there are details here—extraordinary details—which are easily missed. Crucially, what happened to make God change his mind? Actually—nothing. Verses at the beginning and end of the story (Genesis 6:5 and 8:21) say bluntly that humankind was "evil" before the Flood, and evil after it. So what changed? In the terms of the story, God changed, though not entirely. He was "heartbroken" (6:6) before the Flood, and, presumably, just as heartbroken after it.

But after the Flood comes one of the most extraordinary verses in the whole Bible:

" ... the Lord thought to himself, I will not curse the land any more because of human beings *since* the ideas of the human mind are evil ... " (Genesis 8:21).

It's as if the Creator God finally realized what he was taking on in creating a world with human beings in it.

The Bible tells the story of God and humankind. That's its "plot". But its scope and its language are worth spelling out. "Made in God's image, male and female": that is our birthright, our DNA, we might say, from the beginning (Genesis 1:27). But what does that mean? Probably, as exhaustive research has suggested, *our capacity to relate*—a defining characteristic also, according to the Bible, of our Creator. (That, of course, can't be assumed.)

Since the Enlightenment, there has been a popular, but distorted, version of the creation story. Its main theme is this: "In the beginning, God gave human beings *freedom of choice*"—a choice between good and evil. But the story doesn't say that. God didn't *give us a choice* between good and evil. He told Adam about "the tree of the knowledge of good and evil", and forbade him to eat from it. So Adam's and Eve's world is more a world of early childhood innocence. (A parent is unlikely to say frequently to a very young child, "You choose".) As the Bible will go on to say: the real freedom of human beings lies ahead, not back in the Garden of Eden.

Adam disobeyed God and chose evil. So there was loss. As poets and many others have observed, "a glory has departed". The lost innocence of childhood? Or is it more than that?

Like the story of creation, we must now understand the story of "the Fall"—when Adam disobeyed God in Eden—differently from before, in the light of what we now know about human evolution. Put negatively, as the rabbis (of biblical times and since) have taught, from earliest times there has been an "evil inclination" in *homo sapiens*. Over how long a period we can't tell. But news bulletins reveal it every day.

The much-caricatured biblical words "sin" and "sinner" are easily misunderstood too. They don't mean primarily disobeying the rules—especially rules about sex and alcohol. They are more to do with that "glory departed"—or, perhaps, like our freedom, a glory not yet reached. St Paul's preferred word for "sin" comes from the world of archery: falling short of the target. And the intended target? In his view, the glory *of God*—whatever that is. The extraordinary thing in the biblical story is that the Creator always intended sharing that glory with human beings, "made in God's image". The psalm we noted briefly in the Introduction describes our "glory" in extraordinary terms:

You have made us *a little less than God ...* " (Psalm 8:5).

Translators of the AV/KJB preferred to write "a little lower than the angels". It's almost as if the translators were embarrassed or barely able to believe the original Hebrew.[14] In the New Testament, there is similar language, as we'll see. The divine "glory" appears to be different from—or even more than—the traditionally conceived place in heaven. The key, as always in the biblical story, is "made in God's image"—male and female.

It's important to put the two creation stories of Genesis 1 and 2 (and there are two) together, since they complement each other. In the second, God says, "It's not good for the human being (*Adam*) to be alone" (Genesis 2:18). Were we, then, made for love? So it might seem, though, again, we have to reinterpret texts written long before our modern understanding of sexual orientation, like the story of Adam and Eve. This, of course, opens up huge questions which can't be discussed in full here. Perhaps we may provisionally say that the Bible reinterpreted encourages us to explore or discover our sexuality, but not (usually) the freedom to choose it.

That darker theme in the Bible of the "evil inclination" in humans has consequences—for creation as well as for ourselves. The Old Testament prophet Jeremiah pictures creation falling apart:

> I looked on the earth, and lo, it
>   was waste and void ...
> I looked on the mountains, and lo,
>   they were quaking ...

> I looked and lo, there was no one at all
> And all the birds of the air had fled
> ... (Jeremiah 4:23–6).

Jeremiah probably foresaw a foreign invasion. His words sound like the end of the world—and for the tiny country of Judah, it was the end of their world for the time being. The prophet goes on to speak of "the wrath of God" (vv. 27–8). That's difficult language for us. Grief or anguish might be a better word than "wrath" or anger, understood as that of a parent who can't stop loving a wayward child. Surprisingly, perhaps, there's quite a lot about divine grief in the Old Testament. Biblical imagery suggests that God's "wrath" is a kind of spiritual darkness which *we bring on ourselves* because our actions go against the very grain of creation.

Many other biblical texts are resonant with contemporary meaning in the twenty-first century. There is a saying of Jesus which refers to Noah and the Flood:

> Just as it was in the days of Noah, so too it will be in the days of the Son of Man. They were eating and drinking and marrying and being given in marriage, until the day Noah entered the ark, and the flood came and destroyed all of them (Luke 17:26–7).

Like the Old Testament prophets, Jesus used "end-of-the-world" language to say that the nation was facing life and death issues. Yet people continued going about their everyday business! A generation or so after Jesus, in 70 CE, the Romans destroyed Jerusalem and its temple. It wasn't God's punishment, but perhaps it was the consequence of what St Paul, after Jesus, was to describe as Israel's misguided "zeal for God", which boiled over into the Jewish-Roman war of 66–70 CE. A twenty-first-century version of Jesus' saying about the days of Noah might begin:

"They were eating and drinking, growing their economies, neglecting the poor . . . "

We've tended to treat the Bible mainly as a personal guide to the spiritual life, often narrowly defined. But it's far more than this. For example, we've missed the references to the earth and its harvests, to right and wrong ways of looking after the earth (I return to this in Chapter 6). However, how to interpret what the Bible says about "God" is a challenge often overlooked. We easily read into the Bible what isn't there and fail to see what is really there.

God and gods

The "God" portrayed in the Bible is remarkably elusive. We mustn't be misled by its stories in which God plays a leading part, and seems, sometimes, to throw his weight around. The deeper reality is different. As the Jewish scriptures, our "Old Testament", say many times: God hides—himself (or herself; as we're seeing, "God" includes both genders). If God were obvious—after all, God is supposed to be the world's creator—presumably more people would believe in God. But since God isn't obvious, then it's intriguing to think that the Creator's "masterpiece" (Bill Bryson's word) is a creature capable of not believing in the Creator at all, and even of blaspheming and thumbing his nose at God.

The Bible portrays a "God" who can't be defined or pinned down. God is an elusive, indefinable mystery, *not* "a being". The most important reference to "God" in the Old Testament is probably God's reply to Moses' question, "What is your name?": "I am that I am" (Exodus 3:13–14 or "I will be what I will be"). I have long thought that some ambiguous texts in the Bible are deliberately so. Here, what this mystery of God is requires both present and future for a full answer.

In the biblical story, the "living God"—another important description—may show up anywhere. But this "living" God is more than a mystery. God is also experienced as a presence, even a personal presence. The heart of the universe, in this view, is more a "You" than an "It", even though a heartfelt cry in the Bible is sometimes "Where are you?"

The Bible suggests that this "mystery" is the key to the wellbeing of the world; it is the wisdom, or order, which pervades and underwrites creation. By contrast, "idols"—as false gods are often called in the Bible—impoverish human life and damage creation. More particularly, idol-worship usually results in the oppression of the poor. In contrast, the Psalms, and other parts of the Old Testament, suggest that "the living God" enriches human life.

Time and again the Psalms of the Old Testament contrast "God" with gods. More broadly, an "idol" might be defined as anything or anyone which claims so much of our allegiance that it begins to diminish and even destroy us. By contrast, a devotion to the "living" God is always associated in the Bible with a remarkable expansion of life, including, against all expectations, human enjoyment.

So what Christian faith says about creation isn't a proof that God exists, or even an explanation of how we got here. It is the recognition of a *mystery*. Even Richard Dawkins, in his latest book, appears to acknowledge that evolution doesn't explain how things began. As we saw in Chapter 1, Christian belief in creation is belief in a creation *out of nothing*. We didn't invent ourselves, even though we're inclined today to think the sky's the limit. And yet the Bible, surprisingly perhaps, suggests we shouldn't underestimate ourselves.

Two final themes from the Bible to end this section. On the one hand, the mystery of "God" transcends all we can imagine. Nothing can enclose or limit this mystery. The Psalmists frequently refer to the One whose "love reaches to the skies, fills the whole universe" and whose presence pervades all things. Yet they also point to One who has an especial care for people in need. "God" even seems to have a count of creatures other than humans:

> I know every mountain bird,
> Even the insects in the field are mine (Psalm 50:1).

Infinite greatness and personal attention combine often in reference to "the living God", as in one prophet: "God" created the stars, "summoning each of them by name" (Isaiah 40:24).

So there is a life-and-death difference between "God" and gods. All other gods sooner or later drain the life out of us, victimizing the poorest most of all. The real "God", if real, is our breath, our light and truth, and perhaps even our love and life.

Richard Dawkins argues we human beings must "outgrow" God. In post-Enlightenment versions of the biblical creation stories, referred to earlier, "God" is seen as the parent of growing teenagers reluctantly giving them the keys to the house. Otherwise, wouldn't they be forever shackled to their Parent in an immature childhood? But what if "God" isn't in competition with humans at all, but turns out to be a quite different sort of parent? What if God's freedom and power don't threaten human freedom at all, and, instead, show the way to it?

It may well be that, in the modern and postmodern eras, a liberation has been necessary—for example, from old ideas of "God" and of eternal punishment. References to "hell" and "eternal punishment" are far less common in the Bible than we have thought or chosen to believe. In the past, people in power had a vested interest in maintaining such an idea of "God". Karl Marx's understanding of religion as "the opium of the people" was not without foundation. There is much to be said for reading the Bible with fresh eyes.

Evolution's climax?

So perhaps now, in the twenty-first century, the Bible is finally coming into its own. The world has changed far more in the last two centuries than in the previous two thousand. The human race stands at a crossroads. We are in danger of wrecking creation and creating our own hell on earth. As Sir David Attenborough, the renowned naturalist, has recently pointed out, the planet itself will survive. But what of ourselves?

For centuries, some Christians have been predicting that "the end is nigh". It still may be—at least for us humans. But we have, I think, taken too literally the Bible's "end-of-the-world" language. The first Christians may have expected the end of the world in their lifetimes, because of the resurrection of Jesus. Or perhaps they had misunderstood Jesus when he said things like, "There are people standing here who won't die before they see the kingdom of God" (e.g. Mark 9:1). That kingdom didn't obviously come. So was this an example of religious people taking words too literally?

According to the New Testament, however, the end of the world *began* with the coming of Jesus. Its language is very striking. The Church's first sermon begins with a reference to "the last days"—a new phrase which the preacher, Peter, adds to the words of the prophet Joel in the Old Testament (Acts 2). There are similar phrases in some of the letters: "the fullness of time" (Galatians 4:4), "in these last days God has spoken to us" (Hebrews 1:2). One sentence sounds even more impressive now, in the light of what we know about evolution:

"God has made known to us . . . a plan for the fullness of time, to gather all things in him (Christ) in heaven and things on earth" (Ephesians 1:10).

What of the very last book of the Bible, "the Revelation of St John the Divine"? Many of us have wondered whether the Bible would be better without Revelation, with its mixture of bizarre visions and horrendous violence. People have made Revelation the basis for predicting all sorts of things, including the end of the world. Back in the 1970s, some felt sure that references to the number seven in Revelation were sometimes coded references to the then seven-member European Common Market. But later developments have rather spoilt that interpretation. Numbers in Revelation are symbolic: 144,000, for example, symbolizes "a huge crowd which no-one can number" (Revelation 7:9); four is the number of the universe (e.g. 6:1); and six the number of evil—hence the number of the beast is 666 (13:18).

"Apocalyptic" writings like Revelation (and Daniel in the Old Testament) were written for critical times. Revelation was intended for late first-century Christians facing persecution, imminent or actual, either in the turbulent period after the death of Nero (68 CE), or during the reign of Domitian in the 90s. Some of its details are a counterblast to Roman imperial propaganda, as in the portrait of "one like a son of man" (i.e. Christ) "holding seven stars in his right hand" (1:16), and the list of Rome's luxury goods, imported from oppressed territories (18:11–17).

Despite these mistaken approaches, the way forward is not to ignore Revelation, but to read it more thoughtfully. Affluent Christians, colluding with global injustice, untouched by persecution, may think we can manage without it, but Christians living in oppression and poverty tell a different story. And, as often, old texts acquire new significance.

The most important question about the future concerns a future coming (or presence—the Greek is intriguingly ambiguous) of Christ. That remains a traditional article of Christian faith. Most New Testament writings refer to it. As a teenage Christian, sometimes with a guilty conscience, I was troubled by the Gospels' picture of "the Son of Man coming on the clouds of heaven" at the end of time. That cannot now be understood literally. "A cloud" or "the clouds" in the Bible were often a symbol of God's presence—as in the story of Jesus' "transfiguration" in the Gospels. What is more, our modern, science-based understanding of the universe makes problematic the idea of a divine descent from the skies.

Most Christians until recently have believed in such a divine intervention at the end of time—as I did. Many fundamentalists still believe it. But the language and perspective change even within the New Testament. Paul's thinking probably changed (though this is disputed). Crucially, many texts do not picture a future Jesus coming alone, but with "the saints". In subsequent chapters, especially Chapter 6, I shall suggest that "the saints" are, in principle, all human beings. So Paul's language about the future reflects the divine-human relationship which runs throughout the Bible, especially what might have been his last reference to the future:

> The created universe is waiting for God's sons
> and daughters to be revealed (Romans 8:19).

Does Revelation portray the future coming of Christ and the events leading up to it? In the past, many have thought so. But much of its language points to *something which has already happened*; for example:

> Sovereignty over the world has passed to our Lord and his Christ, and he shall reign for ever (10:15).

and

> Hallelujah! The Lord our God, sovereign over all, has entered on his reign! (19:6).

This may sound triumphalist, unattractive, perhaps even threatening, whether we believe in God or not. (What do people singing or listening to Handel's "Hallelujah Chorus" imagine, if they pause to think about the words?) However, one crucial, though bizarre, image (if taken literally) of a "lamb" sharing the throne of God "in heaven" may be the key to Revelation—*a God like Jesus.*

So the book of Revelation may not be about the end of the world after all. But it may portray, like other New Testament writers, the beginning of the end. Or even, in our evolutionary perspective, the climax of creation. Does the Bible teach that God will one day destroy the world? 2 Peter 3:1–13 might suggest so—or would this be another over-literal interpretation? (Even if it did, it would be the odd one out in the New Testament.)[15]

The Bible's leading motif of a covenant between humankind and "God" offers a picture of a bright future for humankind. The Creator takes a gamble on "the universe's supreme achievement"—a "little lower than God" (Psalm 8)—*and* "worst nightmare", a creature whose real freedom and glory lie ahead. But will it all have been worthwhile? That is a fundamental question for humankind and presumably our Creator, too.[16] Both Creator and creature seem to be in for "a long haul".

The Bible's "God", then, sometimes seems to be an elusive mystery: "I will be what I will be." In the meantime, there are false trails: "idols" which diminish, rather than lead humans to their full potential. The future is at least partly open; *crises*, turning-points, moments of "judgement" come and go. The question becomes: has evolution played all its cards? Or is there a clue to our common human future?

CHAPTER 3

Jesus: Truly human, truly God?

Is it possible that "God" is the key to our common future and even the world's survival? For Christians, the questions about God and our common human future go together because of Jesus. According to Christian faith, Jesus was and is fully God and fully human—no half-and-half, no dilution of either, no conflict or tension between Jesus Son of Man and Jesus Son of God (the New Testament Gospels describe him as both). Jesus is one seamless whole. So, if the Bible is the story of God and humankind, then, on this premise, the figure of Jesus is the heart of the Bible—the key, in a way, to the whole story. In this chapter, we consider how his life, death and "resurrection" might shed some light on the questions of ourselves and of God.

Jesus: the enigma from Nazareth

Imagine the impression Jesus of Nazareth first made on people. Though there were rumours about him back home, no-one would have known of what we now call the virgin birth. Whether that is true is not the question to ask here. The humanity and divinity of Jesus don't depend on it, in spite of what many think. Mentioned in only the first chapters of Matthew's and Luke's Gospels (Matthew 1:18–25; Luke 1:26–38), the virginal conception of Jesus, as narrated, isn't meant to "prove" the uniqueness or perfection of Jesus. Nor can it be about biology. That would be to put the story on the level of pagan myths about gods impregnating human women. What can be said is that the narratives are meant to indicate that the birth of Jesus was, in the first place, *God's* initiative.

Imagine, first, the scene at the River Jordan. Jesus, perhaps until now a disciple of John the Baptist, comes to the river to be baptized by his mentor John. According to the Gospels of Matthew, Mark and Luke:

> There came a voice out of the skies: "You are my beloved son … " (e.g. Mark 1:11).

Was that voice audible to Jesus only? Perhaps so. God doesn't seem to operate with that kind of megaphone from heaven. All our experience of how "God"—assuming God exists—communicates with humans suggests a quieter, gentler way of operating—usually in human minds and hearts. Did John the Baptist know who Jesus was? Probably not, to judge from his later question. (On this, see below.)

So what was there to see? A man hailing from Nazareth—the son of a carpenter—being baptized in the Jordan along with everyone else. At this stage in his life, no-one would have thought of him as "son of God" or "Messiah" (God's "Anointed"). If there was a text from the Bible to attach to this still anonymous man as he was baptized, it could have been one from an Old Testament prophet: "He was numbered with sinners"—one of the *hoi polloi* in the Jordan.

This same text was quoted later with reference to his execution (Luke 22:36). So you might say he ended his public life as he began it, though in much more horrific circumstances.

What followed? This Jesus from Nazareth began to make his mark both as a teacher and a healer. His teaching often had a bite and a wit to it. Sometimes he made people laugh about the religious authorities of the day: they strain to get a tiny insect out of their food and end up swallowing a camel. Sometimes he said things which astonished and shocked people: it's easier for a camel to go through the eye of a needle than for a rich person to get into God's kingdom; unless people become like little children they won't get into that kingdom.

There was much more to startle and even shock. He made the member of a despised, hated race the hero of one of his stories—the so-called "Good Samaritan". Another story told of a loving father, but one who contradicted everything a dignified Oriental patriarch was supposed to be—like running to welcome home a wastrel of a son.

Many people recognized that he spoke with "authority". He sounded authentic—made people think about themselves, about life, their nation, and, most of all, about God. Questions about God must have loomed large amongst his audiences. Is God really like that? Who is this "Father" about whom Jesus speaks? Does the authority with which Jesus speaks come from God? And if not from God, then from where?

God questions could hardly be avoided because—and scholars are well-nigh unanimous about this—a leading theme of Jesus' teaching was "the kingdom of God". In contemporary English, that sounds like a place—as kingdoms usually are. But in the Aramaic language Jesus spoke, and in the Hebrew scriptures he would have known, God's reign and kingdom were a way of referring to God himself—all that God is and aims to do as Creator of the world and of Israel.

His "miracles" raised the same kind of God questions. Actually, "miracle" isn't a good word to use. It's not a biblical word. The Gospel writers prefer to write of the "mighty works" of Jesus, or the "signs" he performed. But we would have to be unduly sceptical not to believe that Jesus had remarkable healing powers—even if crowd psychology was a factor in his growing reputation.

So what are we to say about the so-called miracles of Jesus? We can look, first, at the evidence and use our intelligence. The evidence that Jesus healed people is compelling. But he didn't have a monopoly of such "miracles". A near-contemporary, a Greek called Apollonius of Tyana, seems to have possessed such powers. Jesus himself recognized that there were fellow-Jews who performed exorcisms as he did. As for other miracles, such as Jesus stilling a raging storm on the Sea of Galilee and, on one occasion, walking on that sea, some Christians interpret them literally, others think that such stories are meant to symbolize his unique, God-given authority. Christians can agree to differ here. In any case, the New Testament Gospels are a world away from the fantastic, often bizarre miracle stories to be found in some of the gospels not included in the New Testament.

As with his teaching, so with Jesus' healings; there was an "edgy", controversial side to what he did. In that community you weren't supposed to touch people judged by both the "Bible" (the Hebrew scriptures) and by popular opinion as unclean: lepers, menstruating women, foreigners, and agents of the hated Romans. Jesus helped or befriended them all.

Once again, the "God questions" came. Who is this, who thinks he can sit so lightly to our sacred rules by touching unclean people? Is he healing people through the power of God—or through another, darker force? Even his former mentor, John—by now in prison—forwarded a question for Jesus: "Are you the one who is to come?" John probably meant: "Are you the Messiah?" Jesus' reply had a sting in the tail:

"Go and report to John what you hear and see. Those who were blind are able to see. Those who were crippled are walking. People with skin diseases are cleansed. Those who were deaf now hear. Those who were dead are now raised up. The poor have good news proclaimed to them. Happy are those who don't stumble and fall because of me" (Matthew 11:5–6).[17]

The sting in the tail lay in the challenge: "Happy are those who don't stumble and fall because of me." "Stumble and fall" has a religious meaning in the New Testament. Here it implied: people might find what I am doing difficult to reconcile with their understanding of God. As well it might. The over-arching question was: who is the God he is talking about and even claiming to represent?

His life and teaching posed other questions. This teacher from Nazareth, so reticent about himself, a mere human (Son of Man), who, really, was he? And what did he teach about the rest of us, and, especially, about the kind of person a human being is supposed to be like?

The death of God?

That brings us to a question not often asked: who did Jesus think he was? Who Jesus really was, and what later Christian faith preached about him, seems not to have been obvious at all in his lifetime. What is more—unlike the Jesus in John's Gospel—he seems to have been very reticent about himself. He rarely, if ever, talked about himself as "Son of God" or "Messiah" ("*Christos*" in Greek). Either, as with John the Baptist, he left people to draw their own conclusions, or he believed that such titles could only be his when he had fulfilled what he believed to be his God-given task.

Still less did he claim to be God—even if some of the things he said and did might have suggested that he did. Instead—and again, the evidence is very strong—he preferred to refer to himself as "a son of man", "a human being". We might well ask: why should Jesus of Nazareth refer to himself like this?

There was a history to the phrase "son of man". It occurs in the Old Testament, in the prophets Ezekiel and Daniel. It may have had connotations of vocation, mission and suffering. Sometimes it seems to mean just what it implies: "a human being like me"—as when Jesus said "a son of man has nowhere to sleep", and, more startlingly, "a son of man must suffer and die".

It's not easy to say what Jesus predicted about himself. Whatever Jesus may have said about his impending death in Jerusalem, it was probably elaborated by the first

Christians, convinced that Jesus had been vindicated by the God he called "Father". The nub of the matter seems to be this. The life of Jesus, his teaching, his healings, the company he kept—almost everything about him (e.g. why choose *twelve* disciples?)—raised questions about God and human beings, especially his own people, Israel. Does his life represent this God? Does he speak with the authority of that God?

The questions about God and himself as "a son of man" became sharper still with his death. But before we come to those questions, there are a couple of things Jesus said with far-reaching implications for us all—that is, if this distant figure from first-century Galilee has anything at all to say to us today.

First, his opponents in Jerusalem asked him what were God's most important commandments. What did their Bible say? Jesus was very clear: love God with all you've got, and love your neighbour as a human being like yourself.[18] The three great Abrahamic faiths converge in this matter. Second—and he said this further back down the road which brought him to Jerusalem—he threw out a searching challenge to would-be followers: anyone who wants to "save" his life is going to lose it. Conversely, anyone who is prepared to lose his life "for my sake and the gospel's" will find it. After all, why gain the whole world, if you lose your life in the process? There's nothing you can do to get that life of yours back...

Against this background, what do his arrest, trial and death seem to say about us human beings and God—"God" as breath, light and love of our life/world? And, crucially, who "handed him over"—that is, to the people who had him tried, tortured and executed? The New Testament gives three answers to that question: Jesus as good as handed himself in; a disciple called Judas betrayed him; and, thirdly, as St Paul later wrote, *God* "handed over" his own Son.

Richard Dawkins and others have been misled by Paul's words here. They don't mean that God was punishing Jesus or demanding a penalty so that he could forgive our sins. We need to recall (Chapter 2) that in the Bible God is represented as doing everything. So "hand over" is Bible-speak for "God did not intervene". (I return to this question in Chapter 4.) Jesus, too, did not resist what happened to him. He let himself be arrested. He made no serious attempt to defend himself at his trial; his almost total silence was remarkable.

In what follows, it's not easy to disentangle what originally happened from early-Church interpretation. It seems that the first Christians found many texts in their scriptures which seemed to predict—even describe—what happened to Jesus—e.g. "he opened not his mouth ... ". So the Gospel narratives here, especially, are a mixture of historical fact and Christian interpretation which sought to draw out the significance of what was going on.

No serious historian contests the fundamental fact: *he was crucified*. The horrific reality of death by crucifixion is easily obscured by Christian art down the centuries, as well as by altars and gilded crosses in churches today. Even the Gospel writers seem reticent about the details. But, then, all their readers or audiences would know what this kind of execution, normally reserved for the lowest of the low, was really like.

The crucifixion raised the biggest God-question of all. How do you reconcile that shameful, gruesome, prolonged execution with whatever Reality there may be called "God"?

The authority of Jesus and of the God he spoke about belong together. Many people today revere Jesus as a teacher and admire his life. But the fundamental questions raised by the Gospels include these: if this teacher not only spoke about his God, but lived and died for that God, then what kind of God is it who let his "son" be crucified? Since he spoke about "a human being" ("son of man"—i.e. himself), what does that imply about human beings?

The mockery from passers-by at the cross is strikingly the same in Matthew, Mark and Luke, though Matthew has slightly more on this theme:

> Save yourself if you are the son of God, and come down from the cross (Matthew 27:40).

This reads like an authentic, historical memory. Even more so are the last words of Jesus, according to Matthew and Mark (Luke, it seems, chose to omit them—John, too, if he knew them):

> My God, my God, why have you forsaken me?
> (Mark 15:34; Matthew 27:46).

This doesn't read like an invention or an exaggeration. Still less does it fit into the "Chinese Whispers" process which Richard Dawkins, with extraordinary disregard for detail and accuracy, claims to find behind the Gospel traditions about Jesus. Why would the first followers of Jesus make this cry of despair his final words? Here, in its sharpest, most shocking form, is what I have been calling "the question of God". Was, and is, this human being dying slowly in humiliation, nakedness and extreme pain, a revelation of the Creator God—the real God?

The "stumble and fall" word which Jesus used in his reply to John the Baptist's question surfaces again in a letter of St Paul—this time the noun, not the verb:

> ... we preach Christ crucified, which is a scandal [Greek *skandalon*] to Jews and foolishness to Greeks (1 Corinthians 1:23).

How can such a revelation of God—if such it is—*not* cause us all to "stumble and fall"? Doesn't it conflict with most of our inherited or *preferred* ideas of God? People continue to ask, with despairing gaze on the world, "Isn't God supposed to be all-powerful?" Even Christians, as I said earlier, fail to make the connection, and continue to believe in a "god" with little or no connection with the crucified Jesus.

The meaning of the cross

In this section, we explore how a mysterious experience which the first disciples called "the resurrection of Jesus" became for them the answer to the question of God. According to Christian faith, the resurrection revealed the meaning of both the life and death which preceded it, and, through that revelation, the truth about both ourselves and our Creator.

But more "ground-clearing" first. Richard Dawkins classes the resurrection of Jesus as a "miracle". That's another of his category errors. As I pointed out earlier, our word "miracle" isn't a New Testament word. Biblical writers preferred to speak of a "mighty work" or a "sign"—by which they meant a sign *of God*. That is the place to start. In any case, the resurrection can't be classed as just "*a* miracle". The resurrection of Jesus is about God or it is nothing. From the start, it was understood to mean the beginning of the End; in our terms, perhaps, the climax of evolution.

But it's natural to ask, "What happened?" It's also tempting for well-meaning Christians to try to prove the resurrection really happened. They should resist the temptation. That would be like trying to prove the existence of God. It can't be done, and, anyway, a proof doesn't bring anyone to a faith worth having. However, it's not easy to *explain away* the sequel to Jesus' death. As with God, so with the resurrection, Christian faith points to *a mystery*: the promise of a new future for humanity and the world. But that's to anticipate.

The resurrection stories at the end of our four Gospels are the place, above all, where Christians get nervous. This was often true of my students. The differences between the Gospels are alarming to people looking for proof of the resurrection. In reply, it simply won't do to say, "Well, four spectators at the same football match come away with different versions of the same match." That's just a lazy conclusion which pays no regard to the big differences between the Gospels, not to mention Paul's list of resurrection appearances in 1 Corinthians 15:3–8.

This is not the place to go into detail, but two things may help. Start with Paul, and his experience of "seeing the Lord". Even that is different from Paul's experience as recounted in Acts. But the *experience* of Paul and the other disciples is not easily accounted for. This doesn't read like fantasizing or wishful thinking, even if some of the accounts have affinities with the experiences of bereaved people. Believing in the resurrection, for Paul, led to a life of considerable suffering (see 2 Corinthians 11:21–33).

Second, distinguish between evidence and testimony. With evidence we try to establish facts; with testimony, the weight rests on how trustworthy and credible the witnesses are. Improbable as it may sound, witnesses include the testimony of the Church down the ages.

In the end, the truth of "the resurrection" really comes down to the God question: *is God real, and is God like Jesus?*

"Resurrection" is a strange, unfamiliar word to twenty-first-century people. "Life after death" is a more familiar concept, whether we believe in it or not. The first thing to notice is that, in the New Testament—especially Paul's letters—the words "resurrection" and "God" come near to being synonyms. They denote the same mysterious power of life and love which Christians call "Creator" and "God". It's not difficult to see why. A verse in Paul highlights a parallel between creation out of nothing and life out of death:

> ... the God who gives life to the dead and calls things that don't exist into existence (Romans 4:17, CEB)

So the resurrection is as much about God as it is about Jesus. Whatever the resurrection was, it wasn't a miracle like the raising of Lazarus or Jairus' daughter to life again. On Easter Day the Church has always proclaimed "The Lord *is risen*." This English translation of the original Greek of the New Testament means: "The Lord *has been raised*"—that is, *God* raised Jesus from the dead. "Jesus lives again" tells only half the story. God comes into it as well.

The central God-question is still, and always will be, is God real? But now it acquires a new dimension: is God the God of the crucified Jesus? Was the resurrection, in fact, God's "yes" to Jesus—God vindicating all that Jesus had stood for and taught in his lifetime?

Let's step back a moment to the Old Testament Psalms. Their authors—traditionally, one author, David—seem not to have believed in life after death. And yet some of them hovered on the edge of it. Their relationship with God in this life was so real and precious to them—and even more, they believed they were precious to God— how could death possibly be the end?

Some Psalms, as the early Christians came to see, seemed to anticipate the resurrection of Jesus—a renewed life with the God who had meant so much to him and them during this life. Psalm 16, quoted in the early days by Peter in Jerusalem—illustrates this well (Acts 2:25–8; Psalm 16:8–11):

> I saw beforehand that the Lord would
>   be with me forever . . .
> So my heart is glad . . .
> And my spirit rejoices;
> My whole body will live in hope,
> For you will not abandon me to death . . .
> You have shown me the paths of life;
> Your presence will fill me with joy.

This is why the resurrection of Jesus *was* the meaning of the cross. It was God's "yes" to Jesus.

The two major conclusions to which the early Church came are these: the enigmatic, even offensive, life and death of Jesus were illuminated by what followed—what has come to be called "the resurrection". They came to see that Jesus provided crucial clues both to what human beings are supposed to be, and to what God is like. More than that, they came to believe that Jesus was God for us all, God with us all. Neither human evil nor the power of death ultimately defeated him. If this should be true, that would certainly throw a different light on both our personal and our common future.

The cross so interpreted also implies another quite crucial point about God for us in the twenty-first century. It reveals a God not outside suffering but at the heart of it. We'll return to this in the next chapter.

CHAPTER 4

"Outgrowing God" or Growing into God?

If Jesus is what Christian faith claims—a truly *human* being, *and* an "incarnation" of the real God—there can be no-one more significant for our common future. But that is far from obvious. More obvious are the signs that the human race is at a crossroads. Can we survive? Can we make good our devastation of the planet? Can we come together in peace and justice? In this chapter, we look in turn at human developments after Jesus, and the new experience of God behind them. Is it possible that, so far from "outgrowing God", there is an invitation somehow to grow into God?

Being human according to St Paul

Ever since Paul dictated or co-wrote his letters, people have found them difficult. Many think of him as the man who complicated the simple gospel of Jesus. Here, however, I'm working from the opposite premiss: Paul was Jesus' most faithful interpreter.

Actually, did his critics but know it, Paul has been having a "makeover". Recent research has shown that we've got him wrong on many key points. Paul wasn't a misogynist. At the end of his longest letter, Romans, he greets Priscilla (the wife's name comes first here!), a female *apostle* called Junia, wrongly thought for centuries to have been a man, and other women such as Mary and Herodias—more leaders? And he entrusted the letter itself to Phoebe to take—and probably read—to the assembled Christians in Rome.

True, he, or a "disciple" writing in his name, wrote: "Wives, obey your husbands." (I once heard an elderly woman announce, after reading this passage in church, "This is *not* the word of the Lord!") But what else could St Paul have said? *Disobey?* Refuse her husband's sexual demands? Twenty-first-century examples should warn us. The consequences then, if her husband had thrown her out, would have been a life of prostitution or penury or, if she stayed, probably violence and rape or both. Paul's advice was an accommodation to first-century social realities. He would have been horrified at its future exploitation by dominant males.

Even the words "It is better for a man to have nothing to do with a woman" were, it now seems, what the Corinthians wrote to Paul, not his advice to them. (There were no quotation marks then!). He also advised the marrieds at Corinth to make time for sex—there'll still be time to pray. And wife and husband had *reciprocal* "rights" in the matter (1 Corinthians 7:4–5). On the other hand, Paul thought a celibate life less complicated than being married, especially if the world was going to end very soon.

Did he tell women to be silent in church? Probably not. Those words (1 Corinthians 14:34–5) may have been added later, and even if they weren't, they must have meant something like "Don't chatter on the back row." It's clear from an earlier chapter that women in the Corinthian church spoke in tongues. As for the veils Paul expected them to wear (1 Corinthians 11:1–12), many scholars now recognize that the veils were a sign of authority and status, rather than submission.

In all, Paul turns out to be closer to Jesus in the challenges he prompted in a male-dominated, patriarchal culture.

But what of the place of Jesus himself in Paul's letters? The human Jesus seems hardly there at all. There are very few obvious references to his life or teaching. And no references either to the "Son of Man", Jesus' preferred way of referring to himself, as we saw in the previous chapter.

"Son of Man", however, is there in disguise in Paul as "*Adam*". The Hebrew word *adam* means "human being" ("mortal"—"made from the dust"). So what Paul says about Jesus as the "ultimate Adam" (1 Corinthians 15:45) is key to what he says about us all. Jesus is the "*ultimate*" human being: the key to our common future.

Centre-stage for Paul is not a new religion, but "*a new creation*"—a very different "take" on the Church from public perceptions of it today. The new Christian communities were to "trail" this new creation by their mode of life. In particular, they bypassed or transcended some fundamental divisions in the ancient world: between Jew and Gentile, male and female, slave and free (Galatians 3:28).

This was only the start. It has been—still is—a very long road to realizing all this. But there is a slow-burning fuse there in the New Testament—in, for example, what Paul says—and how he says it—to a slave-owner called Philemon in the shortest of his letters contained in the New Testament. I don't want to let Paul off too lightly, but can he be blamed if eighteenth- and nineteenth-century slave-owners quoted him in support of their foul deeds? The likely consequence in the Roman empire for a disobedient slave was crucifixion.

Paul calls the communities he founded not just "churches" but "the body of Christ". That sounds strange, but there was a precedent in standard Greek and Roman teaching about the body politic. In Paul, however, there's a radical difference. Instead of everyone knowing their place—up or down, usually—the watchword in Paul is "one another" (one word in the original Greek). They are to look out for one another: encourage, forgive, pray for one another; be forbearing and generous towards one another.

Paul even describes the command to "bear each other's burdens" as the law of Christ. He is referring to burdens (*bare*) too heavy for one person to carry on their own. Contrast the "pack" (*phortion*) Paul goes on to mention which *is* each person's own responsibility—perhaps that of fulfilling their deepest calling to be a kind, generous human being. "The body of Christ", according to Paul, will reflect this. No member of "the body" should be made to feel they don't belong; none should be so arrogant or intolerant that they say to another, "I don't need you" (1 Corinthians 12:12–27). It's a blueprint, not just for a church, but for the nations.

For Paul, Jesus is *the* "human being" (*anthropos*) who brings life where "Adam"—i.e. the rest of us!—brings death. (If this sounds too gloomy, think of the national and international headlines on an average day.) "The last Adam" becomes "a life-giving spirit" (1 Corinthians 15:45). In all this, Paul comes close to a kind of universalism: God intends, in the end, to save everyone. That, certainly, according to a later writer, is what God wants.[19]

In understanding the Christian faith, and Paul in particular, the word "sin" has been used too much—and misunderstood. Its fundamental meaning in Paul is "shortcoming": we don't measure up to the "glory" we're intended to have (Romans 3:23). If Paul is on the right lines, the ultimate human being, Jesus, points the way forward to our common human future. He is the measure for us all.

If there is some truth in this, then Christian faith is meant to make us more, not less, human. And being human, crucially, means recognizing that we *belong to each other*. So Paul turns out to be a major contributor to one of our key questions: what are we humans meant to be?

But that isn't all that Paul gives us. He borrowed another idea from the Genesis creation stories: Jesus "the image (*eikon*) of God". In this section, we've seen how Jesus fulfils what we might call Adam's "job description", what the Creator intended humans to be. But "image of God" obviously has a second meaning: a likeness *to God*. This will be the theme of our next section.

A god crucified

A teacher once asked her class of young children to draw a picture of God. A tall order, you might think! In Paul's view, I believe, their best response would have been to draw a man on a cross. It's noticeable that when Paul refers to Jesus, uppermost in his mind very often is the crucified Jesus. What might the implications be for our understanding of God—if God there is—if a crucified man is his (or her) image of God?[20] Strange as it may seem, the New Testament implies that the Jesus who "returned" to God after his death now, in that "risen" life, transcends the categories of male and female. It's not how most people—including some Christians—think of God.

Many years ago, we suffered three burglaries in quick succession. On the Sunday after one of them, I mentioned it to a group of people in church after the evening service. One lady, feeling very sorry for us, exploded in indignation: "They should have their hands chopped off!" It seems we Christians can all too readily believe in a God unlike Jesus!

That is easily said, but the implications are huge. For example, would a Christian who really believed that the crucified Jesus is the very image of God support the death penalty, or acquiesce in the nuclear arms race or social injustice? I assume here what the New Testament everywhere implies that the death of Jesus was a summary of everything which he had said and stood for during his life. The death of Martin Luther King might be a modern parallel.

To say, in response, "We have to live in the real world in which all kinds of compromises are necessary", might seem natural. Or is what we think of as the real world something of a distortion, however much we have to work with it and in it? Those of us who live in democracies have less excuse than St Paul in "accommodating to social realities" (my earlier phrase about Paul).

So how does the crucified Jesus as the image of God *par excellence* affect our understanding of God? I suggest we look at Paul—not as we imagine him to be, but as an icon of Christ. That, after all, is what he believed he—and all Christians—were called to be: imitators of Christ. So there is a double reflection going on: *Paul reflects Christ*, and *Christ reflects God* (1 Corinthians 11:1). It follows from this "double reflection" that Paul's descriptions of himself representing Jesus throw a flood of light on his understanding of God.

Almost all these self-descriptions occur in his letters to Corinth.[21] That's probably because the Christians at Corinth seem not to have grasped that the crucified Jesus, *and* his unprepossessing apostle Paul, were, in Paul's view, the image of God. Here are two examples from several which could be given:

> "We (apostles) are fools for Christ, but you are wise through Christ! We are weak, but you are strong!" (Paul had just written about the crucified Christ as "the foolishness" and "the weakness" of God) (1 Corinthians 4:10).

> "Poor ourselves, we bring wealth to many; penniless we own the world." (Paul goes on to write about the poverty of Christ: "Although he was rich, he became poor for our sakes, so that you could become rich through his poverty.") (2 Corinthians 6:10 and 8:9).

So there is a pattern: Paul represents—especially in his sufferings—the crucified Jesus, and Jesus reflects God. This seems highly relevant to the Christian understanding of God. For example, does it then make sense to say that God is "all-powerful"? That God "controls" everything? Or that God could have prevented Covid-19 if he'd "intervened"? What the New Testament—and Christian faith itself—understands by God's "power", "control" and impact on the world needs to be rethought in the light of what Paul saw as God's weakness revealed in a crucified man.

One of the great saints of the Church suggested that God looks at us "lovingly *and humbly*". Similarly, a great nineteenth-century man of prayer, the Abbé Huvelin, once said in a sermon: "You (God) took always the lowest place and did it so completely that no-one ever since has been able to wrest it from you." This is startling stuff, but I suggest that they are clues to what a crucified man as God's image implies.

The New Testament—and many subsequent hymns—might seem to say the opposite, as in "He (Christ) humbled himself... as far as death on a cross. So *God exalted him...*" (Philippians 2:9–10). Many Christians have taken that to mean that the humiliation of Jesus was only temporary; his coming into the world was, as it were, a painful episode in the life of God, but no more than that. In fact, New Testament writers, Paul included, point to something far more radical: in the crucifixion, *intervening* was precisely what God did not do —in spite of the prayer of Jesus himself in Gethsemane. God was already there, tortured and torn apart on the cross of the world. Christian faith has called the whole Jesus event the "incarnation" of God, revealing not only the eternal love, but also the *eternal suffering* of God.

The Bible nowhere says that God the Father punished God the Son in order that he could then forgive our sins. That's our misreading of it. (Richard Dawkins and others assume an "all-powerful" god could have "intervened" to prevent the death of his son Jesus.) Rather, "God was *in Christ* ... making friends with the world" (2 Corinthians 5:19). That's the meaning here of "reconcile". And the suffering involved remains in God's heart—the continuing cost of creating a world.

Two important conclusions follow, pointing to a quite different understanding of God from common assumptions today. First, the cross of Jesus must mean that *God has no enemies at all.* Any enmity between the Creator and his creation is entirely on our side. It also means: no favourite nations now—all are favourites. (Paul devotes three whole chapters—Romans 9–11—to this tortuous subject. There's no basis for anti-Semitism here!) So even though God, according to the Old Testament, began with Israel, that's not where God ended up: crucified in no-man's land. Is it possible that that is where God is to be found today?

In his letters, Paul uses the words "every" and "all" time and again. No exceptions, no exclusions from the grace and love of God. From being a zealous Pharisee who avoided "unclean" Gentiles, Paul devoted the rest of his life to a remarkable—and costly—bridge-building mission between Jew and Gentile because he believed that's what God had done in Christ (1 Corinthians 9:19–23).

In our day of overheated religion and politics, Paul's bridge-building mission is well worth pondering. As a Pharisee, his icon may well have been Phinehas in the Old Testament, who killed the opponents of God (Numbers 26:6–9). Paul criticized his own people for what he saw as their unenlightened zeal for God. Like them, he had always believed in God's "enduring" love, as in the Psalms. But now, because of Jesus and his cross, he believed in God's *universal* love.

The second point which emerges from our understanding of the crucified Jesus as the icon of God is the mystery of suffering. I come back to that at the end of this chapter.

Outgrowing God or growing into God?

Richard Dawkins has suggested that it's time for human beings to outgrow God. Two replies (amongst many) to Dawkins are worth noting. Rupert Shortt has published *Outgrowing Dawkins: God for Grown-Ups*. The subtitle expresses well an alternative to the juvenile caricature of a god offered in Dawkins' book. As we saw in Chapter 1, most human beings, as we grow up, have caricatures of God to grow out of. It can be a lifetime's job to distinguish between our lesser gods and the Mystery which the Bible refers to as the living God. It's unlikely to happen without prayer. A religion, like a marriage or friendship, is something you get to know from the inside.

That brings me to the second of Richard Dawkins' critics. David Bentley Hart suggests that anyone who is serious about the reality of God, including scientists and atheists, should pray—exploration and experience make a vital contribution to the "evidence". This is an intriguing idea, to say the least. But if God is more a mysterious presence than a supernatural force—a "You" rather than an "It"—then inspecting the evidence, as in a science laboratory, is clearly not all that's needed.

In this chapter, I have outlined the two central claims of Christian faith about Jesus as the image or icon of God. As the ultimate human being, Jesus fulfils what we might call "the job spec" of Adam, the mythical figure portrayed at the Bible's beginning as the first human being. But "image of God" also means, as the Jesus of John's Gospel expressed it, "Those who have seen me have seen the Father." That can only mean a Creator as selfless as Jesus appears to have been. His "legacy", we might say, was "Love one another *as I have loved you*."

So the notion that "god" is somehow "jealous" of humans, like Richard Dawkins' caricature, is a pagan idea, not a Christian one. But there *are* gods to outgrow. Human hearts and minds fasten on such gods, which diminish their adherents and impoverish others—especially poor and marginalized people. Contemporary forms of nationalism and capitalism sometimes do so. Our own religious—not to mention political and economic—language can lead us astray. The expression "*our* God" occurs hardly at all in the New Testament. "Our"—even when we mean "the Christian God"—can be dangerously divisive, especially if it implies "*exclusively* ours".

Any god—even with a Christian "label"—which makes its worshippers closed, not open, less human, not more human, cannot be above criticism. No-one should pronounce on whether a person is a Christian or not—unless they are cruel and destructive towards other people. By contrast, a person who puts love first has already begun to encounter the mystery of God.

The New Testament invites us to grow *into* God. Its language, especially in John's Gospel and Paul's letters, is very clear. It talks of living "in Christ" and "abiding in me" (i.e. Jesus). The reference in John's Gospel, often heard at funeral services, to many "dwelling-places" in "my Father's house" suggests there is room in the heart of God for everyone. If that is so, "abiding" in God or "in Christ" in practice seems to mean being open to love and to living thankfully and prayerfully.

Interestingly, the word "Christian" occurs hardly at all in the New Testament.

Many Christians today quote or wonder about a text which appears to exclude people of other faiths:

> I am the Way, the Truth and the Life; no-one comes to the Father except through Me (John 14:6).

This verse expresses the heart of Christian faith very succinctly. But "except through me" isn't the same as "unless you believe in me" or "unless you become a Christian". What those words mean is something we discover through prayer, contemplation and love. In the closely related Gospel and First Letter of John, "love" is key—as is the historical figure of Jesus, because it's through Christ's death for everyone that we know what love really is (1 John 3:16).

So understood, John 14:6 and its "except" clause doesn't necessarily exclude people of other faiths. That can't have been its original meaning. Instead, must we not say that all whose lives are deeply marked by love, kindness and compassion can hardly be strangers to the God whom Christians believe was revealed in Jesus? It shouldn't surprise us that more and more people are discovering that growing understanding and friendships between people of different faiths are life-enhancing, spiritually enriching experiences.

It's true that "a God crucified" remains "a stumbling-block" to adherents of Judaism and Islam. Here theological arguments are probably irrelevant. But maybe the sufferings of the apostle Paul, as an icon of the crucified God, are not. Jewish people, Muslims and others have a right to say to the Christian Church,

"Unless I see the marks of the nails (sc. of the cross) in your hands . . . , I will not believe." Here I adapt the words of a black South African church leader, echoing the disciple Thomas in John's Gospel (John 20:25). In the light of the Church's history, stained by its crusading, anti-Semitic, imperial and colonial past, these are important words for our day.

I return, finally, to the question of God's own suffering—so central to the understanding of Christian faith now. The meaning of the cross needs to be re-expressed for our day, more knowledgeable as we now are about our evolution, and more aware than ever of the suffering and pain in the human world and in creation. The notion that God "sends" suffering is wide of the mark. Pain and suffering are simply there in life and the world, not all caused by humans, though we are responsible for much. They seem to be integral to evolution and the whole creative process. We can feel driven at times to blasphemy or atheism.

It may be significant that the anguish and the anger directed towards God in both the Old Testament and in our world now are largely absent from the New Testament. Christian faith would say that that's because of the cross—testimony to the eternal suffering of the Creator. If there is any truth in this, we are faced, I think, with an existential choice: to declare wholeheartedly for life and the world as we experience them, for other people as we find them, and, in and above all, for love. Alternatives, I suggest, are not as attractive or satisfying as they might appear. Nor, in the long run, do they offer much for our common future. But a wholehearted declaration for life and love eventually leads, in the Christian view, in the direction of God, if indeed the universe's central mystery can be expressed by three simple words: "God is love" (1 John 4:8 and 16).

Behind those words is the conviction that a selfless, non-coercive Creator has made human beings his "heirs". A story Jesus told recounts how a younger son wanted his father dead: "Give me my share of the inheritance," he said, took himself off into a "far country" and squandered it all. Eventually, he set off back home, prepared to settle for slavery. To his astonishment, he came back to a party and discovered he was still family (Luke 15:11–31).

But there was also an elder son in this story, none too pleased at his younger brother's return. People who are moral, conscientious and, sometimes, religious are not always keen to welcome prodigals back home. In the following chapters, we explore what kind of Church is now needed in an emerging new age.

CHAPTER 5

Towards a More Human Church

The twin crises of Covid-19 and climate change present the Christian churches with critical challenges. During the pandemic, churches were in lockdown, services of worship suspended, and access to church buildings forbidden or severely limited. The crisis has been compared with ancient Israel's exile in Babylon, evoking the plaintive cry of Psalm 137: "How shall we sing the Lord's song in a strange land?" So now, will there be a return to old ways of being church? What will be the "new normal", if one at all?

In western Europe and the USA church attendances have been falling. The so-called "developed" world has become a place in which Christian faith and the Church seem marginal and irrelevant. "Church" has begun to appear "old school", a relic from the past: an obstacle to human freedom and progress. If, however, what we need is not a Church going into liquidation, but one renewed and made more human, what does that involve? This chapter explores possible ways forward.

Contemplative and worldly

Many local churches, and many Churches at national level, are too busy and church-centred for their own good. It's all very well for a golf club to be golf-club-centred—what else would it be? But a church-centred church is a contradiction in terms. However highfalutin or vague it may sound, the Church is called to be centred on the "God" it believes in. Instead, at all levels, the churches easily become absorbed in keeping up numbers and, increasingly, on survival. Church buildings take up an immense amount of time and money. So do internal matters of faith and order—especially matters to do with an ordained ministry.

Keeping the Church going is an idea foreign to the New Testament. So too is the notion of "supporting" the Church. Your golf club or your political party may need your support, but not your church—whatever you may think. The New Testament assumes that "God"—if God there is—supports and keeps the Church going. "God", it seems, has other tasks for followers of Jesus. The last thing the world needs in the current crises are churches centred on themselves and their survival.

Both Church and world need a faith which is more reflective and prayerful. But here, too, there is much misunderstanding. For many people, prayer begins as a *cri de coeur* in an emergency, and that, as far back as human beings can be traced, seems always to have been so. Christians often describe prayer as "talking to God".

But is that all it is? Someone recently told me she talked to God all day long. I tried gently to suggest that it was more than that.

Maybe some of us have taken some words of Jesus too literally: "Ask and you will receive . . . ." So prayer becomes a kind of "shopping list" for God. Yet the Lord's Prayer given by Jesus to his first disciples includes "Give us this day our daily bread", and this in a country and in a century when most people lived near and sometimes below subsistence level. So there is a basis in Christianity's foundation documents for "asking" prayers.

Christian praying, in fact, has always been down-to-earth: begin where you are, not where you'd like to be; pray as you can, not as you can't; tell God what is in your heart. ("If something is big enough to worry about, it's not too small to pray about.") Yet prayers aren't always answered when and how we want, as Jesus and Paul knew full well.

Why do we rarely get beyond the stage of telling God what we want? After all, "Isn't that what a god is there for?" Well, perhaps not. A great theologian of the twentieth century, Karl Rahner, claimed that "the fervent Christian of the future will be a mystic",[22] where "mystic" means not someone dabbling in the occult and the like, but someone who engages in a deeper kind of praying—deeper than just asking God for things, however important.

This kind of praying—"contemplative" is a better word than "mystical"—has been thought in the past to be mainly the vocation of monks and nuns only. But today this seems to be changing. Many people, whether religious or not, practise meditation and mindfulness. These disciplines are not in themselves prayer, but perhaps they may help towards a more contemplative way of praying.

John's Gospel often carries on where the other three Gospels leave off. It does so with prayer. "Asking" becomes, in John, "asking in my name": "If you ask anything *in my name* I will do it." Jesus in John says it three times (John 14:13; 15:16; 16:23), but what does it mean?

Christians often take praying "in Jesus' name" or "through Jesus Christ our Lord" to be a sort of pin number which ensures our prayer "gets through". But praying "in my name" really means praying "in Christ"—i.e. "inhabiting" the presence of the Creator whom Christians believe shares our life in Jesus. That doesn't mean we no longer ask or hope for things in our praying. But more is involved.

In the other Gospels, Jesus says not just "Ask and it will be given to you", but also " ... seek, and you will find, knock and the door will be opened to you". The Bible as a whole seems to say that the "God" who is our breath, light and life is the ultimate "object" of our asking, our seeking and "knocking". The fourth-century

Church father Augustine wrote: "Our hearts are restless, until they find their rest in you."

Many of us are understandably hesitant and unsure about this. If God really is like Jesus—the Jesus crucified—then that means an encounter with a selfless Creator. And that's likely to involve a gradual, gentle subversion of our own selfishness. And yet, down the centuries, people have testified to an attractive, magnetic God who is the source of humanity's deepest longings.

This kind of praying, which puts God rather than our "shopping lists" at its centre, will, I suggest, be the beating heart of the Church of the future. Much will follow from it. The Bible will take on a new life. People will read it with more enthusiasm, rather than as a dutiful habit. Churchgoing will be less of a tired habit. Even preaching—its importance so underestimated—will become more alive and human.

But there is a surprise. Contemplative Christians, or—let us say—Christians who aspire to be contemplative, will be more, not less, engaged in the world, more committed to life and appreciative of life. The story of Thomas Merton is worth telling.

An American Cistercian monk, Merton entered his monastery as an otherworldly sort of Christian who looked with some disdain on the world he thought he was leaving behind. As time went by and his life of prayer deepened, his attitude changed. In the 1960s, he opposed the Vietnam War, sounded an early alarm about the environment and engaged with people of other faiths. As he himself wrote, "The true contemplative is not less interested than others in normal life, not less concerned with what goes on in the world, but *more* interested, more concerned."[23]

This engagement with the wider world is likely to be costly to the Church—as it often has been. There were more Christian martyrs in the twentieth century than in any previous one, and the twenty-first century looks like carrying on where the twentieth left off. Contemplative Christians are bound to be led to share in what St Paul called "the fellowship of Christ's sufferings". A Church centred on God is centred on a God crucified at the heart of the world. Members of cloistered religious orders share this through their intercessions—no light or easy "cop-out".

A contemplative way of life embraces everything—especially and above all, marriage for those who are married. It was a Benedictine monk (of all people!) who told me, "You must work out your ministry in the context of your marriage." The church minister whose wife left a note on his desk asking, "Could I have a pastoral visit, please?" clearly had some way to go.

The ripples of a more contemplative, reflective way of life spread far and wide. Our frenetic world surely needs it. The lockdown of 2020 was a culture shock to many, offering a glimpse of a quieter, less pressurized, greener way of life. The future of Sunday could be a useful measure. Of course, we can't go back to a traditional Sunday, associated as it was with "Thou shalt not". Healthier and wiser is Merton's advice: "Sunday reminds us of the peace that should filter through the whole week when our week is properly oriented."[24] In this, as in much else, the great religious traditions of the world have much to share with each other.

United?

The churches are not as disunited as they were. Across the world, previously separate churches have come together; nationally and internationally, discussions continue. And yet many churchgoers are nervous of unity, worrying about a "take-over" or a uniformity in which Sunday worship is the same for everyone. Alternatively, it is sometimes argued, "We may look divided, but it's spiritual unity that counts." (Or does "spiritual unity" mean just being "nice and polite" to one another?) But is that what the much-quoted prayer of Jesus for his followers, "May they all be one", actually means?

We need to hear the full version of that prayer:

> May they all be one, *as you, Father, are in me and I in you, so may they, too, be in us ... in order that the world may believe that you sent me* (John 17:21,23).

This fuller version is crucial in understanding the prayer. It describes a unity *rooted in God*: *the unity of "Father and Son"*—the unity of love because God is love. We in the churches seem not to appreciate the stark implications of this simple truth. How can we draw nearer to the God we all believe in *unless* we draw nearer—in truth and love—to one another? This question can be reversed: how can we draw nearer to one another unless we draw nearer to God? Our snail-like progress to unity may reflect a flawed spirituality—perhaps churches centred more on themselves than in God.

The prayer of Jesus for unity continues: " ... *that the world may believe* ... " *Unless we unite*, the world will not come to faith in the Father and the Son. So the moral imperative could hardly be clearer. What is holding us back?

At the time of writing, in the British context at least, the progress towards unity is stuttering, the pace painfully slow. (As someone personally involved in two ecumenical dialogues for over forty years, I own up to my share of responsibility for this.) Yet the time in which we live is now so critical. The planet is burning. The United Nations, for all its achievements, limps along because individual nations come first. Who will speak authoritatively for the unity and common future of humankind?

Is there any "lawful impediment" preventing a united Church? I know of none. Roman Catholics and Lutherans have put their names to a document which marked the end of a centuries-old argument and misunderstanding about "justification". Methodists and Catholics have explored and agreed upon the extensive common ground they share. The list could be extended. On all the fundamentals of Christian faith, most, if not all, the leading churches are agreed. Why is it that we are still divided by issues of ministry above all? It feels a bit like the tail wagging the dog. Isn't it a reflection of how church-centred the churches are—and perhaps always have been?

Christians within the churches already may disagree with one another about many things: pacifism, their country's defence policy, marriage and sexuality, and much more. So how much diversity can there, or even should there be?

In the early Church the diversity rapidly became extraordinary. (One early picture suggests the opposite (Acts 2:42–7), and I return to that in the next chapter.) Most of Paul's letters and Acts are dominated by the issue of unity between Jew and Gentile in the early Christian communities. *The* issue was whether Gentile converts should observe the law of Moses, so sacrosanct to every Jew.

Paul's "line", eventually received by most, and canonized by its inclusion in the Christian scriptures (our New Testament), was: "Accept one another, as God has accepted you" (Romans 15:7). That is, a converted Gentile did not have to become a practising Jew. So a Gentile man didn't have to be circumcised, or keep the

Sabbath and Jewish food laws, and Peter, James and other Jewish disciples could go on being practising Jews. This was a costly diversity, involving much anguish and searching of consciences. The golden rule was: do nothing to threaten, damage or destroy the faith of another. The grace of God in another person's life can't be denied; to do so comes close to the unforgivable sin.

Paul himself felt called to be "all things to all people"—a self-denying vocation (whatever it may sound like to modern ears) which has been called "the adaptability of love". Imagine a peacemaker in Northern Ireland during the Troubles shuttling between Catholic and Protestant communities, and we get some idea of the suffering, misunderstanding and even violence which came Paul's way in his ministry of unity.

Does this diversity mean anything goes? Far from it. In due course, the historic creeds (Apostles' and Nicene) came to summarize the heart of Christian faith. Within these parameters of Christian orthodoxy (a truly broad, not narrow, concept), love and courtesy require respect for each other's differences, learning from them, perhaps even sharing them. Protestants may discover why Mary means so much to Catholics, and Catholics why the "priesthood of all believers" is so precious to Methodists. (I return briefly to the question of Christian unity in Chapter 8.)

Peter in the New Testament is a key figure. To him, primarily, Jesus gave a commission to be a "rock", a "shepherd", though the other disciples shared the commission. Peter was often the spokesperson for the others—a representative, perhaps, of disciples of the future. But Peter was a flawed character. (Even after Pentecost he was criticized by Paul.) He denied Jesus, though all the disciples deserted Jesus in the end. Earlier, Peter tried to keep Jesus from his cross, earning the searing rebuke from his leader, "Get behind me, Satan." This is another text whose contemporary implications we haven't fully recognized. Here, especially, Peter represents us all. The Church too readily springs to the defence of Jesus and his God.

If we take "Peter" in the New Testament seriously, we are likely to conclude that a united Church needs a visible head. Such a leader will seek to embody the humility, self-denial, love and compassion of Jesus portrayed in the Gospels. Pope Francis has gone a long way towards fulfilling that profile.

Living with questions/A prophetic nuisance

The creeds don't say, "We believe in One ... Prophetic Church." But they imply it; it's there in the Church's DNA. Jesus and the prophets spoke truth to power, above all when the powerful abused their power, as when King Ahab fancied someone else's vineyard, and killed to get it. In our current crises, I suggest we look, rather than for an individual prophet or two, for an entire (church) community which is prophetic.

Prophets played their part in international politics, too. In two crises, Isaiah called king and nation back to fundamentals—i.e. faith in God, and the social justice which went with it. Over a century later, Jeremiah incurred the wrath of king and people alike in telling them to stop dreaming nationalist dreams and, instead, surrender to the new superpower, Babylon. For him, too, faith in God and social justice went hand in hand.

Jesus stood in this prophetic tradition. He exposed what he saw as the hypocrisy of scribe and Pharisee, and put searching questions about their religion and practice to the Sadducees, the party of the establishment in Jerusalem.

Paul and the Church carried on where Jesus left off—at least to begin with.

Prophets ask awkward questions, speak uncomfortable truths. That much is clear. But in what kind of spirit do they speak? Christians have never been sure about anger. When is it justified? Encountering it is usually painful and embarrassing. Angry though Jesus sometimes sounds—and no doubt was—his tears are a surer guide. A word which can't be spoken in love as well as anger, if need be, is probably better not spoken at all.

This is the "Achilles heel" of the Church today. We are often angry *and judgemental*. And that, for a Church supposed to speak in the spirit of Jesus, can't be right. Speaking the truth in love, however hard (Ephesians 4:15), is the golden rule. But that doesn't excuse Christian *niceness*, still less silence when a prophetic word is needed. Being "nice", neither loving nor (apparently) angry, often hides a multitude of sins.

The Covid-19 crisis has exposed what we already knew or should have known: within some countries racial prejudice and the grave injustice arising from it; in many more countries appalling inequalities between rich and poor. And the world's poorest peoples are already bearing the brunt of climate change. In the face of all this, one biblical word stands out: *justice*: "putting right what is wrong". Seeking that justice—God's own mission—defines the Church's prophetic task.

"Liberation theology" was a way of Christian reflection and action which began in Latin America. It sought to embody God's "bias" to the poor portrayed in the Bible, beginning with God's rescue of the Hebrew slaves from the oppression of Pharoah. In my own country, the UK, little is heard of liberation theology. But why? There are great inequalities in income, housing, health and educational opportunities. A growing body of legislation, producing "a hostile environment" for many of other races and nationalities, indulges a narrow British (English?) nationalism, reflected in strident newspapers. Many of the victims of this hostile environment are the very people who have propped up the UK's over-stretched national health and social care services. Some lost their lives in the Covid crisis.

Prophetic Christian witness in Britain has been patchy at best. The heyday of a Christian socialism came and went. But why? As we shall see, there is a basis for it in the Bible. For a time, people said the Labour Party owed more to Methodism than to Marx. (Not that Labour has the sole claim to Christian support.) Between the two world wars, Archbishop William Temple and others worked tirelessly to address acute economic and social hardship, particularly unemployment.

The Covid-19 crisis has brought Britain and many countries face-to-face with some of life's fundamentals: what, as a country, should we value most? And whom should we value—and remunerate accordingly? For half a century and more, we have been brainwashed by the mantra that the profit motive is what oils the wheels of society—if indeed there is such a thing as society. Now there are welcome signs of recognizing that we need each other and that investing in the common good is a good idea after all. Yet bishops have been threatened because the oppressive creed to which we've been in thrall implies that the proper place for religion is the private sphere, not the public square.

A prophetic Church will be controversial and sometimes unpopular. It can't be otherwise; it *always* means a bias to the poor. A more just tax system will lighten the burdens on the poorest at the expense of the richest. Justice in housing involves challenging patterns of house ownership and ownership of land. More than 90 per cent of the land in the UK is in private hands, less than 5 per cent accessible to the general public, and the number of people with two homes—and often more—has been increasing.

The educational imbalance is a long-standing one. Private education, at present, is better than state education, with more opportunities in life for those who are its beneficiaries. Our democracy, too—and others—needs to be repaired with, for example, state funding for political parties, rather than a bias to the rich. Even democracies can be subverted.

To challenge all this is not "the politics of envy", as our more toxic newspapers would have it. It is to get serious about the justice of God, and to join in God's mission in putting right what is wrong.

There are no easy solutions. Powerful forces undergird the status quo; those who have much often resist giving up even a little. My argument is not that the Church should side with this party or that. Nor should it attempt detailed blueprints. But it must speak "truth to power", pose the awkward questions which people in positions of power might prefer not to address, and, in its words and its actions, point to the Creator God whom those in authority might prefer to forget.

Is a prophetic Church likely to be submerged, to go under, beneath the sheer weight of vested interests, opposition or just a suffocating apathy? Not, I think, ultimately. Of all the many dogmas promulgated by the Church down the centuries, there can be few which have been more misunderstood—by Protestants and many Catholics—than the doctrine of "papal infallibility". It was first stated in 1870, a time of acute crisis for the Roman Catholic Church. (The very survival of the papacy seemed threatened by a resurgent, newly united Italy.) What it seeks to safeguard is a belief, shared by all the churches, that the Christian Church cannot ultimately fail because its vocation, to share the gospel of Christ, is a God-given one.

That, of course, begs enormous questions. But, understood in the light of the spirit, light and love which is God, perhaps the Church's vocation might be regarded as trailing, or helping to trail, the way to a more human future. With that in mind, we need to widen the perspective further in the next chapter.

CHAPTER 6

Joining the Human Race

In a private letter written in 1996, a man called Donald Nicholl wrote:

> I believe that the human family will tear itself to pieces unless the whole family learns to love unconditionally.[25]

The current crises of Covid-19 and climate change are making necessary a united world. Medical research needs to be shared, for example, and both Covid vaccines and the patents for them. Climate targets need to be not only agreed, but implemented. These twin crises highlight the dangers to us all. The gods of yesteryear, nationalism and capitalism, have outgrown their value, except where a few peoples have yet to taste independence, and where capitalism with a human face still does more good than harm.

Donald Nicholl, in that letter, went on: "Jesus opened up the treasures of other religions, and . . . the treasures of all creatures who are longing for unconditional love."[26] Against this background, we explore how one religious tradition can contribute to a more global perspective.

A cosmic patriotism: Joining the human race

Marathon-running formed an important part of my life for some twenty years. London Marathons, especially, were memorable occasions because of the sheer number of runners involved. Many thousands congregate each year at the two mass starts at Blackheath and Greenwich. At my level, there was time to talk both before the start and even, for a while, after it, because we were too crowded together to begin serious running. Massed bands and cheering crowds along the way underlined what a richly human experience it was. So, too, did the placards, pinned to runners' vests, which advertised the charity they were running for.

For most of us, there was no sense of competing. (It was very different, of course, for the elite athletes out in front.) At the most, if we'd run a marathon before, we might be out to improve on our personal best time. The London Marathon illuminated for me a remark by one of my New Testament teachers: "Christian baptism means joining the human race."

In one obvious, biological sense, we all join the human race at birth. But isn't more involved? We can live our lives in varying degrees of self-isolation. Being religious might lead us to self-isolate. But Christian faith, properly understood, commits us to the whole human race. Christians have sometimes thought themselves called to be "in the world but not of it". But that's to misunderstand the language of John's Gospel. In that Gospel, Jesus, image of God, commits himself wholly to the world, and disciples living "in Christ" do the same.

How we perceive other people is crucial. A fellow minister and I were sharing a meal in a busy restaurant one Sunday after church. My companion, looking around, remarked to me: "I look at it this way: everyone is in—unless they opt out." Yet the Church—and most Christians—have for centuries believed the opposite: everyone is "out"—an unbeliever, not "saved"—unless they opt in. Yet despite some fierce-sounding texts in the Bible, the biblical view is remarkably inclusive. God's rainbow after the Flood overarched everyone. The rainbow is still there in the last book of the Bible. Two verses are especially clear: God wants to save everyone, because God loves the whole world. I don't mean that believing or not believing doesn't matter. It does. But the Christian faith is still more inclusive than many of us had thought.

Do we have a choice in the matter? Or are we frogmarched into heaven whether we like it or not? Fundamental to Christian faith is the belief that our Creator is not coercive, does not override our free will. But, as the story of the prodigal son makes crystal clear, the prodigal was still family, even "in a far country".

The challenge of the future, whether we are religious or not, is this: if it's true that, at the deepest level of all, love makes the world go round, then our human unity matters deeply. And if love holds the world together because our common Creator *is* love, then how much we love our fellow human beings becomes foundational to our common future. A cameo of what reads like an open-air party sets the scene.

At this party, there was food, enjoyment and friendship in plenty. The party, however, was taking place in a corner of the Temple precincts in Jerusalem. At this party, lasting for days presumably, no-one was left homeless, hungry or needy at all, because they all shared what they had, not just food, but their possessions as well.

This is one of our earliest glimpses of the Christian Church. It was a network of friends; no-one called anything their own, so no-one went without. Maybe they believed the end of the world was near, or, more likely, that the end of the world *had begun*. The Creator God had a future holiday (a "sabbath") planned for everyone, so maybe these folk partying thought every day was a holiday (Acts 2:42–7; 4:32–5).

This may be an idealized version of what happened. The party doesn't seem to have lasted. But the memory and the ideal remained, as Paul's criticisms of the common Christian meal at Corinth showed. In effect, "stop organizing the Lord's Supper as if it's a pagan dinner party, with the poorest on wooden benches outside the dining-room. You're *the body of Christ* for Heaven's sake" (1 Corinthians 11:17–34).

So what changed? Did people get disillusioned? There's no hint of that anywhere. This street party doesn't read like a failed experiment—as if early enthusiasm had led them astray. In fact, this memory of partying every day was clearly not forgotten, as Paul's strictures to the Corinthians show. The picture in Acts 2 became part of the Bible, so is meant to be a kind of measure for the future. Maybe the writer idealized a little. But it stands as a reminder not just of first principles, but of our common future. The Church's central act of worship, often called "Eucharist" (*the* Thanksgiving), describes the sharing of the bread and wine as "a foretaste of the heavenly banquet prepared for all humankind".

In the Christian view, the Church, flawed as it is, dangerous as it has sometimes been and still can be, is necessary to our human future because it bears the heavy responsibility of sharing and living the story of Jesus, the image of both God and "the ultimate human". The timescale has changed. But, as we've seen, with the coming of Jesus a new experience of God and of human community took root in our history.

The "street party" model of Acts 2 and 4 wasn't adopted everywhere. It is not a model to be slavishly imitated—but still a model and an inspiration never to be forgotten. With the coming of Jesus, the world's timetable was reset. All time, from then on, became "the fullness of time", the beginning of the end of the world. The community Jesus founded was meant to be a foretaste of the future. Luke's language in Acts is very telling. Greek ideals of friendship are deployed in this picture of the Church. This is the human community *par excellence.*

So why are many churches so *church-centred*? A leading New Testament scholar has lamented the extraordinary expense, time and effort invested in buildings. Our church-centred language—"supporting" and "keeping the church going"—gives us away; that is Someone Else's job.

The media may give us a skewed picture of the Church. Bad news, they say, sells newspapers. In fact, there are far more good news stories about churches than ever reach the media. Rupert Shortt recently wrote that the Church comprises the largest store of social capital on earth. That is a worldwide, practical outcome of Paul's image of "the body", an image which applies not just to the Church, but to every body politic and the whole human race. The perhaps cryptic title of this section comes from G. K. Chesterton's masterpiece *Orthodoxy*. In a chapter entitled "The Flag of the World", he explains how Christianity invites us to a primary loyalty—to the universe, to life itself. Chesterton calls it "a cosmic patriotism".[27]

The nations and the planet

Since the Protestant Reformations of the sixteenth century, interpretation of the Bible has, until recently, been dominated by the theme of salvation of the individual; for example, is a person "justified" by grace (through faith) or by "good works"? That question remains important. But we are now realizing that the Bible is more this-worldly than we had thought. It begins with creation and ends with a vision of "a new heaven and a new earth". Jesus instructed his disciples to pray, "Your kingdom come *on earth* as in heaven."

Until the twentieth century, life for most people was "nasty, brutish and short" (Thomas Hobbes). Survival in this life, and a place in heaven in the next life, dominated most people's agendas. Now, as more people are being lifted out of poverty, and more people live longer (with serious exceptions to both these advances), we are noticing new dimensions in the Bible's message.

Even Paul was not as other-worldly as he's often made out to be. His collection for the poor in Jerusalem, gathered from his Gentile churches, was not just a powerful ecumenical statement, but a sign of human solidarity. "The nations" (*alias* the Gentiles) are a major theme in both Old and New Testaments.

Not only "the nations" are prominent in the Bible. So, too, is the earth. To begin at the beginning, not only did God create it, the earth remains his. God hasn't detached himself from it, or limited his role to being the keeper of human morals, especially sexual ones.

The Old Testament offers several visions of a world in peace and justice. Two prophets, in almost identical words, envisage a united, peaceful world centred on "Zion" (i.e. Jerusalem); others are more universal. The New Testament offers a picture of a Christ-centred world, but still an inclusive one. In such a world, there is no place for narrow nationalisms. In the age of European empires and colonialism, peoples under foreign rule naturally wanted independence. But now, when an independent nation continues to make nationalism a rallying-cry, the results are likely to be toxic. Who is the enemy now? All nationalisms need an opponent, whether a foreign enemy or "an enemy within".

Patriotism is rather different, but, as Edith Cavell, the British nurse of World War I, famously said, "Patriotism is not enough." And why not? Because loyalty to, and love of, one's country need a deeper loyalty and deeper values if they are not to turn toxic under pressure. Instead, the human race now needs Chesterton's cosmic patriotism. In religious language, our primary loyalty and love under God is the human race. We are created by God, so constitute one family. A proper understanding of Christianity points to a "united nations". What theological or moral sense does "Britain first" or "British self-isolation" make? That remains an urgent question for a country which has just exited the

European Union. Nostalgia and fond memories can lead a country down a dangerous cul-de-sac.

In most of its visions of the future, the Bible portrays nations united in their praise of God (e.g. Psalm 67). There is a similar perspective on "the earth". The Bible's starting point and end point are:

> The earth is the Lord's, and all that is in it (Psalm 24:1; cf. Genesis 1).

> I saw a new heaven and a new earth (Revelation 21:1).

The psalm could hardly be clearer: all land belongs to God. (The words in the original Hebrew and Greek mean both "earth" and "land".) The world seems to have lost sight of this. I recall a public notice in Wales referring to "the owners" of the River Wye. There were no doubt important fishing rights at stake. But God has everywhere become the invisible, disregarded landlord. The results have been disastrous.

Many biblical texts describe the human trashing of God's earth and its consequences. The prophet Jeremiah, as we saw in Chapter 2, saw "a reversal of the creative process, an undoing of the work of God". The gathering darkness shows that God is "unmaking" his creation.[28] A later verse expresses what is amiss:

> ... your wrong doing has upset nature's order,
> and your sins have kept away her bounty
> (Jeremiah 5:25).

Compare the psalm which refers to a Creator who

> ... turns rivers into desert,
> springs of water into parched ground;
> He turns fruitful land into salt-marsh,
> *because the people who live there are so
> wicked* (Psalm 107:33–4; cf. 35).

Biblical writers, as we've seen, had no concept of secondary causation, but that doesn't mean that God is disconnected from God's world or that our actions don't have consequences. If we don't believe in a punitive god—and I suggest we shouldn't—how are we to understand this connection between wrong-doing and a creation unravelling?

According to the Bible, human idolatry is the problem. Taking the real God for granted or ignoring God has far-reaching effects on us, even if those effects are slow-burning and invisible to begin with. Something replaces that deepest loyalty and love for which we were created. As the Greek philosopher Aristotle said, "nature abhors a vacuum"—and that includes a spiritual vacuum. Our attitudes to ourselves, to other people and to creation—especially under pressure—may slowly change. Substitute "gods" are not always obvious, but they are nonetheless real, with dire long-term effects: they make their devotees less than human, distorting their priorities, rendering the neediest invisible; they ravage the earth and its harvests; they oppress the poor.

It's not being far-fetched to make a connection here between this biblical picture and a rapacious capitalism which ravages the earth in a ruthless quest to maximize profits. This is a capitalism, of course, from which millions of us have benefited. Yet its effects have also lulled us into an amoral and immoral sleep.

Two problems cry out for our urgent attention:

1. the very unequal sharing of God's earth—acute in my own country, and, no doubt, many more.
2. the strain upon the planet of human use and misuse of the earth and its resources—including, of course, the seas.

Where is the justice in all this—justice for all the creatures with whom we share the earth, as well as justice among and between members of the one human family? God's justice means putting right what is wrong—and in the Bible this is not simply postponed to an afterlife. It's often down-to-earth, as in one prophet's dream of a world put right:

> Each man will sit under his own vine or his own fig tree, with none to cause alarm (Micah 4:4).

So what of property rights? The Ten Commandments forbid both stealing and "coveting"—i.e. taking or even wanting what your neighbour has. That is a red line if we are to avoid anarchy and social disintegration. Property rights are rightly enshrined in law. But does that put them above question and contradiction? Some think so. There is a church website in America which proclaims a kind of "holy trinity": "faith, tradition *and property*".

But what if "the neighbour" has far more than he should have, even if he's worked hard for it and earned it? What if he has so much that his neighbours (i.e. his fellow human beings) are driven into poverty? The world's richest people—though some are great benefactors—often make it their business to fund and elect a party which will look after their wealth. Even in democracies they fund the likeliest party.

Yet the Bible's portrayals of the Creator's justice cannot be construed as socialism or communism, words which in our day have become terms of abuse. Christian realism has tended to say: pray for the wisdom to change what you can, and to accept what you can't change. But that easily slides into accepting the status quo, even when the status quo is blatantly unjust and unsatisfactory. Of some things it may be said: "That's impossible to achieve on earth." But can that be said of the project *of the Creator*—even the Creator with *homo sapiens* as a flawed and sometimes reluctant partner?

Hope in the Bible has deep roots. So far, I've hardly mentioned creatures other than ourselves. But the

Bible is not as human-centred as we have thought. We share the earth with other creatures. God made it for them, too (Genesis 1; Psalm 104, e.g. vv. 16 and 17). We humans don't even get a day to ourselves in the seven-day account of creation at the beginning of the Bible; we share Day Six with all other living creatures. As for human "dominion", we are increasingly realizing that means responsibility for looking after creation and all its creatures, not exploiting it or driving to extinction fellow-sharers of the earth.

We believe in life before and after death . . .

Christian faith and interpretations of the Bible have been changing over the last half-century and more. That is only to be expected. All the time we are learning new truths about the world we live in and gaining new perspectives on both the Bible and the faith. But what of older emphases, particularly beliefs in life after death and the last judgement? In most previous centuries, these tended to dominate the Christian horizon. Preachers and teachers threatened congregations and schoolchildren with the threat of hell fire, and since life was so short and uncertain, what happened after death loomed large.

Some years ago, Christian Aid adopted the strapline "We believe in life before death". It was a welcome—and challenging—corrective to the long-standing preoccupation with death and the afterlife. So much so that now these subjects are rarely mentioned. They are increasingly airbrushed even out of funerals. But a book about God and our future can hardly pass over them in silence.

The New Testament message about death is clear. God in Jesus overcame it, and therefore so shall "we". But who is the "we" here? We've noted that the Bible, despite its sometimes threatening and exclusive-sounding language, has a vision which is remarkably inclusive. ("Everyone is 'in', unless they opt out.") Several Psalms strike a positive note about "the nations", so often condemned in the Old Testament. The picture of the "new Jerusalem" in the Bible's last chapter includes trees beside the river of life "with leaves for the healing of the nations".

So does the final judgement, as it's been called, amount to a cursory "nod-through" at the proverbial pearly gates? "We all get there in the end"? Rather more needs to be said, simply because both the Bible and Christian faith say more.

The Bible presents us with an insoluble conundrum. It can be expressed in the form of two questions:

- Will God ever give up on anyone, regarding them as a lost cause?
- If not, will God ever override someone's free will, saying, in effect, "You're coming to heaven whether you like it or not"?

It seems to me that the Bible says or implies "No" to both questions. God won't give up on anyone. Nor will God frogmarch anyone into heaven against their will. Hence my insoluble conundrum.

It may help to put down one or two markers. I recall a conversation with a student about freedom of choice. (It was, interestingly, in Mrs Thatcher's heyday as the UK's prime minister.) The student was quite clear: if you choose Christ, you are saved; if not, you are destined for hell.

Some people continue to believe a version of Christian faith rather like that. I countered then, and still would now, by pointing out that life is anything but a level playing field. Some people are far more likely to become Christians than others. Even when we have recognized that we don't make ourselves Christians in the way that we might choose how to vote, it's still true that some are more likely to become Christians than others. God is not morally credible if, in whatever final judgement there might be, it's the same "exam paper" for everyone. ("Did you believe in Christ? If so, welcome. If not, sorry . . . .") Far more challenging is the picture of that "final exam" in a parable of Jesus (see Matthew 25:31–36) in which practical compassion seems to be the be-all and end-all. But even here there is something unsettling and subversive. Both the "sheep" and the "goats" sound surprised at their welcome and rejection respectively by "the king".

A saint of the early centuries said that in the evening of our lives we would be examined in love. A notable Christian historian counselled against pictorializing God sitting on a judgement seat: "Some people would hold that sitting in judgement on men's sins is not a first-class occupation for a first-class God." He goes on to suggest that such a picture in the Old Testament comes from earlier, pagan sources: "The more exciting parts of the Old Testament portray a God who has a distinctly gentle side in dealing even with terrible offenders."[29] The New Testament goes even further in portraying God as "drawing sinners to him" by the power of love. I suspect that many of our pictures of a stern judge at a final judgement include projections of our own anger against people who appal or disgust us.

Yet a bland universalism is not where the Bible ends up. It's uncompromising from start to finish in what it says about "the wicked". It is severe on rich people who have gained their wealth at the expense of others, on the powerful who have abused their power, and on anyone who ill-treats those to whom life has dealt a difficult hand ("the widow and the orphan"). Will they be simply "nodded through" at the end? We should not presume to judge, and maybe in the end we have to fall back on a "staged" approach to heaven, not unlike the medieval understanding of purgatory, or the Buddhist understanding of karma.[30]

Yet we reap what we sow. The Bible is clear about that. "God will destroy the wicked," say the Psalms time and again. But the cross suggests that the defining characteristic of the love of God is "overcoming evil with good" (Romans 12:21), and God will leave no stone unturned to bring everyone home.

Two definitions to conclude this section: the nearest the Bible comes to a definition of "the judgement" is the verse we noted in Chapter 1: *the* judgement is preferring darkness to light *when the light has already come* (John 3:19), to which we should add: "Now is the judgement"—that is, when the Light and Love in the person of Jesus are crucified (John 12:31). So judgement means "sifting"—the wheat from the chaff, for example. A good deal of sifting is going on now. Is that spirit, light, love, which some call "God", nudging us, as history accelerates "in these last days", towards a better, more human world?

And also this definition: "Judgement is whispering into the ear of a merciful and compassionate God the story of my life which I had never been able to tell"—if we can bring ourselves—or are given the grace—to do that, whether now or in an afterlife.[31]

We shall need to return to this in a later chapter.

CHAPTER 7

God and Life

You're still not convinced about God? I don't blame you. There is much in life and in the world to engender doubts and questions. And you're still, perhaps, doubtful about, or critical of, the Bible. Yet it can't be said too often: there are better ways of thinking about "God" than some traditional Christian ideas and outdated interpretations of the Bible.

For example, the Bible in its entirety doesn't give us a picture of "God" who is a control freak or a bully, nor a disconnected, detached god. Rather, "God" is the breath or spirit, light and truth, life and love at the heart of everything. They are the key to many New Testament texts. Paul, speaking to Greek intellectuals in Athens, refers to the God "in whom we live and move and are" (Acts 17:28). In his letters, or in letters in his name, he writes in similar vein of

> (the God) "from whom and through whom and for whom all things exist" (Romans 11:36);

(the God) "whose purpose is everywhere at work" (Ephesians 1:11);

and the one (i.e. Christ) whose "fullness" is filling the universe in all its parts (Ephesians 1:23).

Strange language, perhaps, for us today. But, according to the Bible, this is the "God" whose presence permeates all things, including ourselves. The themes of this chapter naturally follow.

Time

A verse in the Psalms has a particular resonance for our day:

... When you (sc. God) rebuke
   anyone to punish his sin,
You make what he desires melt away (Psalm 39:11).

The original Hebrew isn't entirely certain, but I have opted for the REB translation. I'm attracted to it because its words seem particularly accurate for two things greatly prized by most people in the "developed" world, and further afield still. These two things are time and money—brought together in the potentially disastrous equation "time is money". I recognize that for many people that equation may be an economic reality, causing them enormous pressure. Yet I still want gently to press the question: should our human life be entirely shaped and determined by time and money?

In Chapter 1, I suggested that we human beings have adopted a "container" view of time. We pack into each day as much as we can. "Pack" is a telling word. We measure the value of a day by how much we've done. "Saving" time is another odd expression. How do we do that, and for what purpose? The eye-wateringly expensive HS2 project in Britain is meant to save time. We've been building bypasses and motorways for half a century—mostly to save time.

Yet the more time we "save", the less we seem to have. Journeys are shorter, but still not likely to be short enough. White vans will still career along our roads to meet schedules and targets. As the poet W. H. Auden wrote, "We are lived by powers we pretend to understand". There is something elusive, even recalcitrant, about time; it doesn't bend to our will.

There is a similar problem about money. Economics isn't the sole cause of our problems, and so unlikely to be the sole cure. It is not a neutral science anyway, affected as it is by attitudes and values, not least trust and integrity. So what *is* the problem? I don't mean that the more we save, the less we seem to have. Often, however, the more we have, the less we think we have, because we can always see someone with more money than ourselves. And the more we have, the more there is to worry about. I'm not implying for one moment what I once heard in a church synod: "A bit of poverty will do us all good." But again, money, like time, doesn't always bend to our wishes. To judge by headlines, and the sheer space and time devoted to it in our media, money is always a problem.

Our attitudes not only to time and money, but also to work, raise important questions. Do we overvalue hard work? Political leaders are constantly praising "hard-working tax-payers". What does that imply about the many people who don't or simply are unable to work? What if the point of life is not so much work, but a rest—what the Bible calls a Sabbath?

Of course, most of us have to earn a living. The science of economics is doubtless important. But is it as important as we have allowed it to become? In the UK, the property and housing market has become an obsession. We are forever taking our economic pulse, and the price of housing, the level of inflation and the cost of living are three key barometers.

"We have to live in the real world." I hear the words in my brain as I type now. But the so-called real world is often taken captive by values and ideologies which are a snare and a delusion. The words of Jesus whisper the real truth: a person's life doesn't consist in how much they have. It might be unhelpful to quote that from a pulpit of a church in the poorest part of the country. Yet Jesus seems to have said those words in a country and at a time when most people lived most of the time near subsistence level.

There are some signs that we are relearning a deeper, older wisdom. A recent book has a telling title and subtitle: *How Much Is Enough? The Love of Money, and the Case for the Good Life*.[32] Its authors define a number of "basic goods" indispensable for a properly human life: health, security, respect, having the space to be yourself ("personality"), harmony with nature, friendship and leisure. Religion, defined as "concern for the ultimate order of things", is also included.

Christianity affirms all of this, especially "the ultimate order of things". That involves paying attention to ourselves and what really helps us all to flourish. But it goes deeper. What is our real glory? It's important both to avoid underestimating ourselves *and* to be realistic about our human tendency to mess up. We sometimes aim for the good but achieve the opposite. And yet some simple practical ways towards the good life can be taken.

As we pursue the good life, including the common good, it's worth asking what is the relationship of God—supposing God is real—to time? It is a question which has taxed the greatest minds! I hope a biblical perspective, plus a definition of a mysterious word, may help.

One of our problems with the mystery of "God" is recognizing that God is both in time and beyond time. The Psalmist declares: "From everlasting to everlasting you are God." A New Testament writer writes in similar vein: "In the Lord's sight one day is like a thousand years and a thousand years one day." That brings us to the mysterious word "eternal". Its fundamental meaning in the Bible seems to be "without beginning or end". But it's not the same as "everlasting", since "eternity" by definition is beyond time. Yet there are hints in the Bible, and, I think, intimations in our own experience, that "the eternal" mysteriously impinges on, embraces and permeates time.

Small wonder that some scientists confuse "God" with a "first cause", or whatever it was which prompted the Big Bang. But here I want to be more practical. What does Christian faith and wisdom teach about time? Here are extracts from a Christian reflection on time in strikingly lyrical, poetic language:

> Trust time. Time is music, and the space out of which it resounds is the future . . .

> Entrust yourself to the grace of Time . . . Time is at once a threat and an unheard-of promise. . . . Time is . . . the grand school of love . . . The ground of our existence is love . . . love is life that pours itself forth.[33]

Poetic gobbledygook, you may think. Or is it possible that our economics-dominated world has lost the poetry and the music of life? If it has, and if, mysteriously, eternity impinges on time, then doesn't this give time—every moment of it—a special significance and value? To make the most of time, you have to "inhabit" the present moment. There is a place, of course, for remembering the past. That can be a creative, life-enhancing experience. There's also a place for thinking about, and planning for, the future. That, too, can be life-enhancing, as well as—sometimes—necessary.

Yet, when we've acknowledged all that, perhaps time, life and God—so Christians would say—form a mysterious unity. To recognize this is an important step towards a more reflective, contemplative way of life. We can all live in the present moment more than we do. Many find the practice of meditation or mindfulness helpful. From the Christian point of view, the discipline of prayer is essential—and not being discouraged by failure is equally essential!

What may we find in the present moment? Certainly more than we might think.

> The present moment is always full of infinite treasure. It contains far more than you have the capacity to hold. Faith is the measure . . .

"Faith" here could be a misleading word. Better, perhaps, to say "trusting"—trusting life, love, God . . . —is key to unlocking the treasures of the present moment. The same writer goes on:

> Love also is the measure: the more your heart loves, the more it desires, and the more it desires the more it finds.[34]

Behind that conviction lay the Christian belief that there is no moment at all in which God is not present, even when that moment may involve suffering. But—and it's an important caveat—we may not know *at the time* that God is present.

As humankind moves into uncharted, uncertain territory—the aftermath of the pandemic and the growing climate crisis—we may perhaps respond to future challenges more creatively and humanly if we can reset our attitudes to time and money.

"Always and everywhere"/Life's rich tapestry

A book called *Children's Letters to God* includes some very appreciative ones: "Last night's sunset was cool—do that again." And, always, honest ones, like: "How do you feel about people who don't believe in you? Somebody else wants to know."

Young children see the world with fewer illusions, prejudices and preoccupations than the rest of us. The poet William Wordsworth may have exaggerated and idealized by his words to the Child who is "Father of the Man", but he surely had a point. Jesus said: "Unless you become like little children, you won't see the kingdom of God—i.e. life."

Young children don't take so much for granted as adults tend to do. It changes as the years go by, when we fail to see, for example, the extraordinary beauty of an oak tree in spring or a beech tree in autumn. We become too busy, preoccupied or anxious to notice. We take life itself for granted. Worse still, we may take other people for granted or even fail to notice them.

Receiving kindness and love from another is to have an intimation of God:

> Everyone who loves is a child of God and knows God, but the unloving know nothing of God, for God is love (1 John 4:7–8).

This is the fundamental reason why the questions of who "God" is and what we are belong together.

Many of us naturally wonder. What any of us believes is never a straightforward choice, seldom clear-cut. Yet the reality of "God" as perceived in Christian faith is deeper and more pervasive than we may think: "closer to us than we are to ourselves". Another verse from the Bible expresses it differently: "Christ in you (or, amongst you), the hope of coming glory" (Colossians 1:27; 2:2). Is this another way of saying that being human is more important than being religious, because God is more human than any of us? Christian faith measures being human by the self-giving love of God in Christ.

This love doesn't distinguish between sacred and secular, as if there are parts of life which are "holy", and parts which are not and never can be. The biblical canvas is as wide as life itself, because God is deeply connected with the whole of life—including human life. As we are seeing, evolution, modern psychology and other undoubted progress in human life are all giving a new lease of life to the Bible. So, too, current crises are pushing us to interpret the Bible in new ways. But to do justice to our humanness, we need to talk about more than love, key though that is.

Recently, I conducted the funeral of a man who, throughout his long life, had been not only a devoted Christian, but also an able singer and musical conductor. He was recognized by everyone who knew him as a warm-hearted human being. Yet no minister can assume that everyone attending a funeral these days believes in God. We shouldn't refer simply to "God" as if everyone knows what we're talking about. So where should we begin?

There is an argument in the Bible which goes like this: if God made the human eye, then God must be able to see; if God made the human ear, then God must be able to hear (Psalm 94:9). The argument needn't surprise us. The Bible begins by telling us that God made human beings in God's own image. (Bill Bryson, quoted in Chapter 1, refers to humankind as "the universe's supreme achievement".)

Of course, taken too literally or too far, that biblical argument is absurd. God transcends all our words and images of God. And yet maybe the Psalmist's argument can be extended. Human beings have a sense of humour. Laughter, when not at someone else's expense, is often attractive and enriching. Do humour and laughter somehow have their origin in a "Creator"?

The title of this section, "always and everywhere", deliberately echoes a phrase in Christian prayer books. Being thankful "always and everywhere" is the Christian ideal. It's the opposite of taking life for granted. At my primary school, we used to sing the hymn "Glad that I live am I". The first line expresses well something quite fundamental to the good life.

Being thankful all the time, of course, is hardly possible—except, perhaps, for a saint. Life is tough for many people—sometimes well-nigh impossible—which is why humans need to look out for each other, and not indulge in a self-isolating thankfulness. If we do, our thankfulness is likely to morph into something less attractive, like selfishness and self-indulgence.

True thankfulness can be cultivated, beginning with making the most of each day as it comes along. When that begins to happen, we have, according to Christian faith, taken an important step towards believing in our Creator. And, to return to an earlier theme, if someone says, "I believe in singing and music as a vital, worthwhile part of human life", isn't that, too, a step in the direction of "God" or God?

"The World is Yours"/Enjoyment

Years ago, I had travelled to preach at a small chapel in the east of England. (Happily, I can no longer remember exactly where.) Just before the service, in the church vestry, I asked the steward who had welcomed me whether anyone came to the chapel from the new housing estate nearby. A disapproving look came over her face. "No," she replied, "all they're interested in is pleasure!"

There is something, alas, in those TV caricatures of religious people after all. The theme of this section is quite the opposite of that sad remark. A three centuries-old Church "confession" tells us what the purpose of human life is: to love God and enjoy God forever.

And with that enjoyment of God (of which, more in a moment) comes the enjoyment of life, the world and other people. Dietrich Bonhoeffer, as often, got it right: God the Creator provides the "bass melody", which is the foundation for all the other melodies of life. It's as Paul said: "Everything is yours ... " What Paul meant by these intriguing words, and what he believed their foundation to be, I return to later on. But, first, a look at—and a listening to—the world around us.

During the first Coronavirus lockdown, my wife Rhiannon and I were entertained by the singing of a blackbird each evening on the chimney of our house. Because we live in a bungalow, and our lounge has an open fireplace, its song came wafting down the chimney clearly during the day and particularly in the evening. It was a wonderful "evensong".

Thomas Hardy's poem, "The Darkling Thrush", describes "an aged thrush", "frail, gaunt and small" singing on a bleak winter's day. There seemed "so little cause for carolings", and the poet cannot but think that the bird's "happy good-night air" betokened:

> Some blessed Hope, whereof he knew
> And I was unaware.

So with our blackbird. When we really listen to the song of birds or look at a tree coming into leaf or a tree in its autumnal glory, and so much else around us, there is much to enjoy. Wordsworth, even if at times he felt "a glory departed" in the world of nature around him, could still write of

> A presence that disturbs me with the joy
>   Of elevated thoughts; a sense sublime
> Of something far more deeply interfused,
> Whose dwelling is the light of setting suns . ··

It's a great pity that biblical translations sometimes—perhaps inevitably—fail to do justice to the richness of the original Hebrew or Greek. The Hebrew word usually translated as "good" in Genesis 1 can also mean "beautiful": "God saw all that God had made and saw that it was beautiful." In one of Paul's letters, the same applies: the Greek word translated as "good" can also mean "beautiful".[35] Biblical faith is far more world-affirming than we have realized; it embraces not just moral truth, but all that's beautiful in creation and in human life. One unsung hero of the Bible—hardly noticed at all—is Bezalel, "skilful in every craft, a master of design", all of which the writer attributes to the Spirit of God (Exodus 31:1-6).

No argument of mine can prove the existence of God, and it would be foolish and presumptuous even to try. But believing in God is not Alice in Wonderland's believing in six impossible things before breakfast. A possible first step is simply being thankful for all that each day brings and trying to put as much of ourselves as we can into what we have to do each day. Easier said than done—yet strangely life-enhancing.

And, finally in this chapter, enjoyment. In the twenty-first century, we are beginning to rediscover a writer of whom—as with the Bible—we might say "his time has come". (I referred briefly to him in Chapter 1.) Thomas Traherne was a priest and poet of the seventeenth century, born in Herefordshire in England. (There is a side-chapel dedicated to him in Hereford Cathedral.) A modern editor of extracts from Traherne's writings wrote:

> The story of this gradual discovery of more and more of Traherne's work is so strange and full of unlikely coincidences that one can hardly help

> wondering whether Traherne will not prove to be one of those writers who wrote more for subsequent ages than for his own. Like Julian of Norwich ... [36]

Traherne's *Centuries* express his glorious vision of life and the world. In them enjoyment is a prominent, recurring theme:

> You never enjoy the world aright, till you see how a sand exhibiteth the wisdom and power of God ...
>
> You never enjoy the World aright till you see all things in it so perfectly yours, that you cannot desire them in any other way ... For can you enjoy anything a better way than in God's Image?[37]

If that sounds selfish, we would be wrong:

> ... You never enjoy the world aright, till you so love the beauty of enjoying it, that you are covetous and earnest to persuade others to enjoy it.[38]

This enjoyment experienced by Traherne (and, I'm guessing, by St Paul—in spite of everything) is rooted in the mystery both writers refer to as "God". What a pity that the Church and Christian tradition haven't always done justice to this "human God" in whom is the secret of our own humanity. In the words of the "confession" of the Church quoted earlier, the purpose of life is: "to love God and enjoy Him forever".

To return to Paul's "motto": "all things are yours" is expanded in what follows: Paul himself, Peter and Apollos... the world is yours. So are life and death. The present and the future are yours—everything is yours. That is indeed, we might think, "everything". You can't get more comprehensive than that. But there is more: a *crescendo* to finish: "And you are Christ's and Christ is God's" (1 Corinthians 3:21–3).

Paul was writing to Christian disciples in Corinth in southern Greece. But, if my argument in this book is on the right lines, that community in Corinth was meant to be a "trailer" for the whole human race. Paul's words suggest our Christian perspective has often been too narrow. The scope of God's Spirit is as wide as life and the universe. The Spirit meets people not only in religious spheres but everywhere—in the natural world, in the give-and-take of relationships, even in the systems that structure human life. "No nook or cranny is untouched by the finger of God. His warm breath streams towards humanity with energy and life."

In a nutshell: "The Spirit... is the life of the life of all creatures; the way in which everything is penetrated by connectedness and relatedness..."[39]

Conclusion

"We believe in life before and after death" was the title of a section in our last chapter. The words "eternal" and "eternity" can bamboozle, even scare us. St Paul is worth quoting once more: "God has prepared things for those who love him that no eye has seen or ear has heard … " (1 Corinthians 2:9). But before that, there are more down-to-earth things to think about—and enjoy.

CHAPTER 8

Embracing and Shaping the Future

Our three questions won't go away. What are we human beings? "The universe's masterpiece" and its "worst nightmare", according to Bill Bryson; in biblical language, we're "a little lower than God" and also the "Adam" who's not yet attained his intended "glory". Could God not have done better? We can speculate. But here we are in a world we haven't made, and the world and life itself require a response. So do our poorest neighbours.

And who or what is "God"? What difference does that make? The three great Abrahamic faiths—Judaism, Christianity and Islam—speak in differing ways of one, all-merciful, all-compassionate God. The Jewish scriptures, the Christian Old Testament, testify to a mysterious personal presence who beckons us into the future and promises to meet us there.

Christian faith has much in common with Judaism and Islam when it speaks of God. But it also speaks of one unique human "incarnation"—the Jesus who fulfilled "the human" which Christianity supposes the Creator dreamed of before time and space began. "In the fullness of time" ("in these last days"), Jesus brings evolution to its fulfilment and goal. His legacy of love—divine and human—might be said to turn evolution on its head and the world upside down. Or perhaps we might think of it as evolution's great leap forward.

It is difficult to get our minds round this. Jesus of Nazareth came preaching:

> "Whoever will save his life will lose it; whoever will lose his life for my sake will find it."

The implications are mind-boggling if, as Christian faith claims, Jesus was and is God in human form. It presumably means God practises what Jesus preached. There's not one rule for God and another for the rest of us. For God, as for us, "Whoever loses his life, will find it ... ". This is the mystery of love, human and divine. "There is no greater love ... "; "this is how we know what love is: Christ died for us."

Christian faith is about an utterly selfless Creator, or it is nothing.

The incarnation welded together Creator and creature, God and humankind, in such a way that the tragic split between the universe's "masterpiece" and its "worst nightmare" could be healed for good. The biblical image of Jesus at "God's right hand"—i.e. at the heart of the universe—is our common future (our third question). All are included—unless we insist on opting out. In the words of the traditional marriage service: "What God has joined, let no-one put asunder."

God, in the mystery of God's own selflessness, has chosen to join the human race—to the point of public humiliation, acute suffering, God-forsaken darkness and death. This, I believe, is why New Testament writers seem untroubled by the God-questions which trouble us: "How can God permit all this pain and suffering?" "Could not an almighty God have created a better world?" Once allow that the cross of Jesus wasn't a passing episode in the life of an eternal God on a fleeting visit to the world, then either the cross is a kind of blasphemy or it is a revelation of the Creator's own enduring suffering.

So what are we? Maybe we begin to find that out by engaging with the Love which initiated, watches over, and leads a creation onwards into its purposed future. How, then, should we now respond to present crises and, in these crises, renew and sustain both ourselves and the world? What might our common future be?

Waking up and getting real

Current crises have been driving many of us back to basics. Much has changed or begun to change in a very short space of time. What will "a new normal" in the future be like—if there ever is a new normal? Life is unlikely to be the same ever again. In all this uncertainty, what landmarks or guideposts might there be?

I have suggested that wisdom is a blind spot in our economically dominated, globalized culture. Clever, skilled, well-informed people we recognize and value. But a *wise* person? What might a wise person contribute to the economy?

It was once very different. Religions and cultures prized wisdom; philosophers and poets encouraged human beings to seek it. A wise person knew himself, could see into the heart of things, knew what really mattered in life, and what their community really needed. Such a person lived by life's deepest values, contented and at peace, without being smug or unengaged with the world around them. But what has been happening to us—especially in the twentieth and twenty-first centuries?

In an accelerating world with so many distractions, we have had little time to reflect upon the fundamental mystery of life itself, the silent event of being. This is what one of the great Christian commentators of our time, David Bentley Hart, had to say at the end of his impressive exploration of "God":

> Atheism may really be only a failure to see something very obvious ... ours is a culture largely formed by an ideological unwillingness to see what is there to be seen ... The reason the very concept of God has become at once

> so impoverished, so thoroughly mythical, and ultimately so incredible for so many modern persons is ... because of all the vital things we have forgotten. Above all ... we have forgotten *being* (my italics): the self-evident mystery of being ... Human beings have never before lived lives so remote from nature, or been more insensible to the enigma it embodies.[40]

The "god" which many atheists criticize and deny rarely, if ever, corresponds to the "God" of the world religions, and certainly not the God of Christian faith. At the same time, it is hardly surprising that people find it hard to believe in a personal God in an increasingly impersonal world. Living in communion with the world, with each other and with God belong together: we can't live with one, but not the others.

So what guideposts might we find as we seek to renew and sustain ourselves? One of the New Testament's most frequent commands is this: "Keep awake". In the past, many thought it meant "Keep alert for the end of the world." But words of Jesus to his disciples seem to rule that out: it's not for us to know. And, anyway, what earthly use would his disciples be if that's all they ever thought about?

"Keep awake" in the New Testament presupposes that we've woken up. Stories of healing and the language of baptism in the New Testament are suggestive of people waking up from the sleep of death or from sleep-inducing darkness and illusion. So this command seems to mean: "Wake up to life, to yourself, to other people and to God."

Waking up to God might seem the key to waking up to everything else. If God is real, then it is clearly fundamental. But in the world we now live in, it may be that many people will come to believe in God *after* they have woken up to themselves, to other people and to life. This is not to marginalize God. But if there is something in Christianity's conviction that God is the breath of life, our light and truth, and the love which makes the world go round, that must mean that all roads to truth and to love lead ultimately to God.

What might waking up to ourselves mean? Wisdom down the ages has taught that an "unexamined" life is not worth living. Waking up to ourselves includes waking up, not just to a greater self-knowledge, but also to our potential—gifts and opportunities we hadn't noticed or found time for. Waking up to the reality of other people is likely to follow. Introspection or self-improvement becomes a limited, sterile exercise if it begins and ends with ourselves.

Waking up to the big wide world, wonderful as it is, also brings its challenges. It can be frightening, especially if, for the first time, we begin to notice what damage our species has inflicted on the planet and what suffering we inflict on each other. So whilst downtime and leisure have their place in any balanced life, resolutely or carelessly shutting our eyes to the reality around us is another matter. That is to sleepwalk to disaster.

Truth-telling and keeping alert to what is being said are an integral part of that. Biblical texts once again can speak with new authority. Two Old Testament books, the Psalms and Jeremiah, warn of those who deceive the people with lies. Jeremiah condemns false prophets who declare "all is well" (Jeremiah 6:14) when it clearly is not. He denounces those who mislead the people with false, nationalist dreams (7:25–32). Psalm after psalm warns of the dangers of the tongue, and of people who say, "By our tongues we shall prevail" (Psalm 12:4). Revelation's fiercest language is reserved for the devil, traditionally "the father of lies". An Old Testament colleague of mine once remarked that one sign of the "darkness" which in the Bible is often a symbol for God's "wrath" is when governments start to believe their own propaganda.

If human beings are to flourish, we have to be able to trust one another. One foundation for that is being able to distinguish real news from fake news, truth-telling from half-truths and propaganda. Our media, too, especially newspapers with rich, powerful owners who want to extend both their wealth and power, need to be regulated without being stifled. We need media outlets which are free, responsible and accountable.

In all of this and much more we need wisdom. In the biblical view, the foundation of wisdom is God:

> The fear of the Lord is the beginning of wisdom (Proverbs 1:7).

"Fear" is an accurate, but misleading translation. "Awe" and "wonder" are nearer the mark. Begin with awe and wonder at the very fact that we're here at all, that the world is as extraordinary as it is, that every day is a gift. All this may help us grasp the direction in which the Bible is pointing us.

As often, the New Testament fills out the picture of "wisdom"—startlingly, in fact, in the figure of a broken man on a cross, *the* place where God and *homo sapiens* meet. This crucified Jesus, according to St Paul, is the wisdom of God. It suggests at least this: that no-one is wise unless truly humble and selfless—the very characteristics of the crucified God.

Dietrich Bonhoeffer, widely acclaimed as one of the great Christians of the twentieth century, was executed by the Nazis in April 1945 for his involvement in the resistance to Hitler. In a letter written to his friend, Eberhard Bethge, on 16 July 1944, Bonhoeffer argued that the way both to truth and the future is the words of Jesus:

> You will never find life (the kingdom of heaven) unless you change direction and become like little children (Matthew 18:3).

Paradoxically, he went on to suggest that humankind has "come of age". That involves abandoning a false conception of God and "a clearing of the decks for the God of the Bible, who conquers power and space in the world *by his weakness*".[41] Might this revelation of God be key to our humanness and a renewed world?

Hoping

I write as an optimist married to a pessimist. It makes for a good partnership. In the famous illustration, an optimist sees a glass half-full, the pessimist sees it half-empty. Who is the more realistic?—the perennial question! Yet both contribute to life's rich tapestry, and whichever we all are is largely, I think, a matter of temperament and genes.

But optimism isn't the same as hope. Optimism is hoping for the best, hoping that what you want to see happen will happen. Real hope is something deeper.

Traditionally, Christian hope has been defined—or caricatured—as "pie in the sky when we die". But just as we must now say, "We believe in life before as well as after death", so now we hope for "the kingdom of God" on earth *as in heaven*—"the community of all human beings in a society of perfect justice and peace, the global village ... "[42]

Much follows from this. Because Jesus, God in human form, embodied the Kingdom of God, Christian hope has both a divine and a human foundation. Again, just as "waking up to life" doesn't necessarily begin with "waking up to God", so hope may begin in and amongst human beings before finding still deeper roots in God. Communities in deprived parts of England are becoming more hopeful again, with signs of social and economic regeneration. That is because a few people—sometimes just one or two—have refused to give up hope, *and have taken action*. They have, for example, helped to create a community hub, or persistently sought new money and, not least, formed teams of helpers who have also refused to give up.

This brings us to an important characteristic of hope, and especially Christian hope. In practice it means believing that nothing which is wrong or unjust is, *by that very fact*, inevitable. Rowan Williams, former Archbishop of Canterbury and now, significantly, president of Christian Aid, in a recent interview, asked: "Why should I take for granted how the international finance system works . . . ? Why should I assume this is a law of nature? Perhaps it is a good idea to ask: do we want to be locked into this? And if we don't, what can we do about it? *Just raising that question is a sign of hope*."[43]

Hope is foundational to the Christian view of things. But it's not a coincidence that "Do not be afraid" is another very frequent command in the New Testament. No-one concerned for the state of their country, or the world, can escape moods of despondency and despair. We have to be realistic about that; the Bible, as always, is. But the "default" position of Christians is faith, love—and hope.

If, then, believing *because of God* that evil and injustice are not inevitable, then neither poverty nor calamitous global warming need be inevitable. Hope is the ground of a revolutionary attitude to the world—a call to a confident journey from the present to the future.[44] This is quite the opposite of what many people—and many Christians—think about the Christian faith. It does *not* support uncritically the establishment or the status quo, particularly if the status quo supports, colludes with or ignores injustice.

Christianity has always had revolution in its bloodstream. It's there in the Song of Mary the mother of Jesus:

> (God) has brought down the powerful
>   from their thrones,
> Raised up the lowly,
> Filled hungry people with good things,
> Sent rich people away empty (Luke 1:52–3).

This version of Acts captures the spirit of early Christianity well:

> Those (Christians) who are turning the world upside down have now turned up here (Acts 17:6, AV/KJV).

The time is ripe for revolution—always, in the Christian view, peaceful and non-violent, but still a real revolution. The times are critical.

Caring for the planet must now mean far more than individual efforts such as abandoning the use of plastic bags, necessary though that is. It involves challenging governments and vested business interests to change direction radically. Christians who are serious about this will find themselves in unlikely, even unsettling, partnerships with people who don't necessarily share their faith. Extinction Rebellion and its supporters, young and old, is a case in point.[45]

The circles of people upon whom Jesus pronounced a blessing extended way beyond those who were his overt disciples and followers. They included peacemakers, those who are merciful, and those who long for and even suffer for a world where justice and the Creator's will are heeded.[46] All such people are grounds for hope. They are people of action who have not accepted as inevitable something which is clearly wrong.

Sometimes, alas, the question, spoken or unspoken, asked by Christians and churchgoers about prospective allies is "Are they one of us? Do they share our faith? Do they refrain from swearing? Dress properly? Will they fit in if they come to (our) church?" As I argued in Chapter 6, Christian faith involves raising "a flag for the world".

There is another word of revolutionary hope which needs to be said as one who belongs to a still disunited Church. There is nothing necessarily wrong with difference amongst Christians, or even separately organized churches, as long as their separateness doesn't hinder the kingdom of God. But that is a crucial, and now highly relevant, caveat.

The central act of Christian worship for most Christians has been and continues to be the Eucharist (called also, for example, the Mass or Holy Communion). It is the thanksgiving *par excellence* in which congregations share bread and wine both in celebration of Jesus and in memory of him. Here, above all, the Church symbolizes and anticipates what the Church points towards: a human race reconciled and at peace in the kingdom of God. So it is a scandal "that the churches to this day do not accept each other in the community of love that they celebrate in their Eucharist".[47] Many readers will know which churches are at fault here. They include the largest in the world and—perhaps—a few of the smallest. Only church-centred churches can regard this as normal. It is wrong, so not inevitable.

Caring

Christians use the word "love" too much. Preachers fall back on it sometimes when they don't understand the Bible reading. (Moral generalities from the pulpit are the death of preaching.) Here I take for granted what previous chapters have argued: love makes the world go round because love is its heart—an unimaginable selflessness, an unconditional love behind and at the very heart of the universe.

Here, I use the word "care"—and for this reason. Way back in the 1960s, an American scholar suggested that the first chapter of Genesis has had a disastrous effect on the planet, and that in two ways. It has encouraged the idea that creation was there "for the benefit of humans", and that God's gift to humankind of "dominion" encouraged abuse of the environment.[48]

The challenge of averting catastrophic global warming remains. The whole human race will need not only to learn wisdom, but also to practise care for the planet and all its creatures in ways and to an extent we have never done before.

Recent research, curious as it may sound, confirms some words of Jesus: a person's "life" doesn't consist in how much they have. Beyond a certain level, necessary to make the most of life and enjoy it, wealth will not enhance our happiness. Caring for each other, and for creation, will. Current crises are showing that God's creation is a unity—or must be, if it is not to destroy or irremediably damage itself. We can't say "Britain first", and pretend Africa isn't there. We can't go on burning oil and coal, keep using toxic pesticides, tipping waste into the oceans, and imagine that creation will somehow take care of itself. Fishing and air travel are two of many human activities which now need to be cut back and strictly regulated.

Two particular groups of human beings need our care and attention now more than ever. One is the up-and-coming generation who will reap what we and others before us have sown. We can't think only about our national economies today and tomorrow, and not how life will be for them in 2050 and beyond. There are no easy solutions, and none which will not involve hardship for many. But the deepest wellbeing (*shalom*) of each is intimately connected with the deepest wellbeing of all, not forgetting the tiniest insects.

It is time to enfranchise the next generation: to share power with them in ways which previous generations did not. In a fast-changing, endangered world, it is their right. And their privilege, as members of the coming kingdom of God. (As for a church without young people, that comes close to being a contradiction in terms.) The "bottom line" in all this is "the earth is the Lord's" (Psalm 24:1) before it is anyone else's.

The second group of people who need the human family's special attention are the world's poorest people. Christian churches have spent a disproportionate amount of time on moral issues such as human sexuality, marriage and divorce. The passions and divisions they have engendered reveal much about where our hearts often are. Our moral preoccupations are out of all proportion to the Bible's overriding concern for the poor, the hungry and the oppressed. Some Roman Catholic theologians of the twentieth century called this "God's preferential option for the poor".

The Bible is very clear about the "agenda" of the mysterious, ever-present Creator God. Psalm 146:5–9 provides a succinct summary:

> God deals out justice to the oppressed.
> The Lord feeds the hungry
> And sets the prisoner free.
> The Lord restores sight to the blind
> And raises those who are bowed down;
> The Lord loves the righteous
> And protects the stranger in the land;
> The Lord gives support to the
>   fatherless and the widow,
> But thwarts the course of the wicked.

How God "thwarts the course of the wicked" isn't always clear; the Bible, and especially the Psalms, often suggest that bad people bring about their own downfall. St Paul echoes a proverbial commonplace—often, though not always observed in human experience, people reap what they sow (Galatians 6:7). He prefaces it by saying "God is not mocked." At the same time, the Creator continues unrelentingly to overcome evil with good, and the eternal heart of that story is the cross of Jesus the Christ.

Conclusion

The Bible time and again contrasts "the living God" with lifeless idols. Idols drain the life out of people and victimize the poor. The living God gives life to and humanizes people. God is not obvious, often elusive. We have made "God" too much of an object, a being, when the truth is more dynamic, more relational. The only three words which the Bible ever uses to "define" this mysterious, personal presence are: breath or spirit; light (and truth); and love. If God really is God—above, beneath, within, amongst, behind everything and everyone—then we can say *God's* breath brings into being and pervades all things; *God's* light and truth are inextinguishable and inescapable; *God's* love is almighty and invincible.

In an age of crisis, questioning and doubt, and in societies which in many ways have become more impersonal, it is not easy to believe in a personal God. Yet Christianity's central icon, the cross, is, in part, an image of God-forsakenness. The Creator practises neither control nor coercion; God's power and sovereignty have to be understood differently. God, as Bonhoeffer saw, comes to us in weakness. A relational God—the Christian icon is a "Trinity"—invites our participation in renewing the earth. A much misunderstood and sometimes maligned Christian leader put it like this:

God is as God is in Jesus. And that is our hope.

And a Personal Postscript

Emerging out of a national pandemic is proving a messy, disorienting business. Will there ever be a new normal again? The urgent questions multiply. Somehow our economic life has to be renewed. People have to be able to earn their living. Yet there are deeper questions.

I began a jigsaw during the first lockdown. It's a map of the British Isles in 1715, with patriotic and military-looking coats-of-arms round the edge. Eventually, I completed it. (The last one was "adjourned" and placed on its board beneath the settee, where it remained for several years.)

Putting "Britain" together in a jigsaw is one thing. How will we put or bring together and renew the real thing? How does any country renew itself? Not just economically, but socially, morally and spiritually as well. We need depth, direction, each other—as well as wealth. Or is "wealth" really the right word? No-one actually *needs* wealth, do they?

There are pressing questions about a way of life often driven by the toxic equation "Time is money." Will we come to look back on previous decades as the age of the commuter? All those hours spent travelling! All those traffic jams! There must be better ways of organizing human life. As the poet plaintively asked, "Where is the life we have lost in living?"

And what of our dysfunctional housing market? So many with two houses and more, so many with none, even allowing for renters who don't want to own their own home.

And aren't things like land, education and even taxation common goods to be shared more fairly? What better way could there be of organizing human life than around common goods such as these? To do so wouldn't be communism, or even socialism, but simply our shared human future, as we leave behind the law of the jungle, the survival of the fittest.

Surely we can leave behind capitalism and nationalism as we have known them. Both are in danger of outliving their usefulness, great as it has been. More benign successors may continue, but it's time to move on: time for a golden age of united nations. That should be part of a new normal, as natural as it is necessary. Whether or not we believe in a Creator who, as the Bible narrates it, has put us all here to share the planet, here we are, and many things are conspiring to make us act like the one human family we are. As there have been very many millennia preceding our arrival on this planet, so there may yet be more ahead of us.

Our neighbourhoods and communities, as well as our countries, can be renewed. We are "wired" to be social, relational creatures, our faces, for example, so expressive and sensitive. A virtual presence is better than an email; the real presence is best of all. Friendships and good conversation are our social bread and butter.

Marriage, too—even if now more varied in our understanding and experience—is a vital part of this picture. The lockdown has been a good experience for my wife and me—though I know full well it has put countless families under enormous pressures. In spite of everything, there is much to be said for the Roman Catholic understanding of marriage as a "sacrament". At its heart it is irreducibly personal—even holy and sacred.

Some are using current crises to reset their lives. It is surely time to stop measuring and evaluating each day by the standard of how much we pack into it. That is the old "container" view of time. Better to greet each day as a gift if we can, and to make the most of it as thankfully and generously as we can. And if the day ahead looks forbidding, can we somehow find the grace to receive it with both hands, and allow it, in spite of its threatening face, to become a blessing? "Grace", like "inspiration", is almost a religious word; both denote something which comes from so deep inside ourselves, it might almost be a gift from somewhere else.

That brings me, finally, to the question of God. It's not surprising people have found it difficult to believe in God in recent decades and centuries. This had been developing for a long time. But, like injustice and so much else, it's not inevitable. Perhaps if, in a new normal ahead of us, we find each other and the natural world around us again, we shall discover even more: that mystery, that spirit, that illumination, that deep love for everything and everyone which Christians call God.

Will the Church be part of the new normal? I hope and believe so. The human race needs the story of Jesus, and our Creator has entrusted a community of flawed human beings (who else did God have to turn to?) with the task of handing it on to future generations. Only let the Church aspire to the full humanity of its Founder. As my Franciscan friend once remarked, "It's more important to be human than religious." If Jesus is to be our guide, then humanity and religion merge into one.

Notes

[1] *The Transforming Friendship* was one of many books written by Leslie Weatherhead, a popular Methodist preacher of the mid-twentieth century.

[2] Eric James, *John A. T. Robinson: Scholar, Pastor, Prophet* (London: Collins, 1987), p. 306.

[3] Rowan Williams, "Analysing atheism: unbelief and the world of faiths", in *Faith in the Public Square* (London: Bloomsbury, 2012), pp. 281–91, quotation from p. 281.

[4] Bill Bryson, *A Short History of Nearly Everything* (New York: Doubleday, 2003), p. 423.

[5] Quotations from the Bible are taken from the REB (the Revised English Bible), unless otherwise stated or my own translation.

[6] The word "god" has traditionally been given a masculine pronoun (he, him, etc.). But if we're to do justice to a transcendent Creator of all, supposing there is such a reality, we need to acknowledge that such a Mystery can be referred to as either "he" or "she".

[7] Neil Richardson, *God in the New Testament* (London: Epworth, 1999), pp. 63–87 (Ch. 3, "When the Image Fades"); see also my *Who On Earth is God?* (London: Bloomsbury, 2014), pp. 93–8 ("Wrath: God's Dark Side—or Ours?").

[8] Bryson, *A Short History*, p. 422.

9   Brian Greene, *Until the End of Time: Mind, Matter and Our Search for Meaning in an Evolving Universe* (London: Allen Lane, 2020), p. 150. Compare Stephen Hawking's "The human race is just a chemical scum on an average-sized planet . . . ." (quoted in Rowan Williams' *Being Human* [London: SPCK, 2018], p. 20).

10 D. Bentley Hart, *The Experience of God: Being, Consciousness, Bliss* (New Haven: Yale University Press, 2013), p. 175 Emphasis in the original.

11 Hart, *Experience of God*, p. 220.

12 Daniel Defoe, *A Journal of the Plague Year* (London: Falcon Press, 1950), e.g. p. 260.

13 Romans 1:18–32 (see the earlier discussion in the Introduction, and the references there).

14 The Hebrew word here for "god" is *elohim*. But although it's plural, it is the word often used in the Old Testament for God. So translations vary: God, gods, angels. But if the thought here reflects the creation story of Genesis ("made in God's image"), "God" may well be the best translation.

15 2 Peter was almost certainly the latest New Testament book to be written. Nearly all scholars are agreed the disciple Peter couldn't have written it. There is a similar problem about 2 Thessalonians 1:6–10: probably not by Paul himself; it certainly seems to conflict with what he says elsewhere, especially in Romans. On these literary questions which affect how we understand the Bible's authority, see the Introduction to my *Paul for Today* (London: SCM Press, 2008), pp. xiv–xvi.

16 In the case of God, how can we be sure what God "thinks"? We Christians are often too confident about that!

17 I quote here from the Common English Bible, an American translation of 2011.

18 Mark 12:28–34; Matthew 22:34–40; Luke 10:25–8.

[19] 1 Timothy 2:4. The majority of scholars have concluded that the letters written to "Timothy" and "Titus" were letters by a later disciple or interpreter of Paul. (The language style and—to some extent—the theology are very different from the letters which Paul himself dictated or co-wrote).

[20] 1 Corinthians 1:18–25 and Philippians 2:5–11 are especially important; their references to weakness, foolishness and shame reflect the horror and public humiliation, as well as the cruelty and agony, of this form of execution, reserved for those deemed the lowest of the low.

[21] 1 Corinthians 4:9–13, 2 Corinthians 4:7–12 and 6:3–10, plus Philippians 3:4–11 (paralleling 2:5–11), are especially revealing of the apostle as an icon of the crucified Jesus.

[22] Quoted in W. Johnston, *The Wounded Stag* (London: Collins Fount Paperbacks, 1985), p. 40.

[23] Thomas Merton, *The Inner Experience* (London: SPCK, 2003), p. 147.

[24] Merton, *Inner Experience*, p. 138.

[25] D. Nicholl, *The Beatitude of Truth: Reflections of a Lifetime* (London: Darton, Longman & Todd, 1997), p. xvii.

[26] Nicholl, *Beatitude of Truth*, p. xvii.

[27] G. K. Chesterton, *Orthodoxy* (London: Hodder & Stoughton, 1996 [1908]), pp. 91–114.

[28] H. McKeating, *The Book of Jeremiah* (London: Epworth, 1999), p. 45.

[29] H. Butterfield, "The Originality of the Old Testament", in *Writings on Christianity and History* (Oxford: Oxford University Press, 1979), p. 85.

[30] P. Knitter, *to be supplied*.

[31] Cardinal Basil Hume OSB, *To Be a Pilgrim* (London: St Paul's Publications, 1984), p. 228.

[32] Robert and Edward Skidelsky, *How Much Is Enough? The Love of Money, and the Case for the Good Life* (London: Allen Lane, 2012).

[33] Hans Von Balthasar, "Heart of the World", in Edward T. Oakes, ed., *German Essays on Religion* (London: Continuum, 1994), pp. 245–56.

[34] Jean-Pierre Caussade, *Self-Abandonment to Divine Providence* (London: Collins, Fontana Library of Theology and Philosophy, 1971), p. 56.

[35] M. Bockmuehl, *The Epistle to the Philippians*, 4th edn (London: A. & C. Black, 1997), p. 250. Bockmuehl calls Paul's language here "truly remarkable"; "Paul's message here is that the mind of Christ does not stand aloof from an accessible vision of beauty, truth and goodness."

[36] A. M. Allchin, *Landscapes of Glory: Daily Readings with Thomas Traherne* (London: Darton, Longman & Todd, 1989), pp. 7–8.

[37] c.38, Thomas Traherne, *Centuries* (London: Mowbray, 1960), p. 18.

[38] c.31, Traherne, *Centuries*, p. 15.

[39] Dale B. Martin, *Biblical Truths: The Meaning of Scripture in the Twenty-First Century* (New Haven: Yale University Press, 2017), pp. 237–8, quoting Clark H. Pinnock and Elizabeth Johnson.

[40] David Bentley Hart, *The Experience of God: Being, Consciousness, Bliss* (New Haven: Yale University Press, 2013), pp. 328–9.

[41] D. Bonhoeffer, *Letters and Papers from Prison* (London: SCM, 1953), pp. 123–4; my italics.

[42] W. Pannenberg, *Christian Spirituality and Sacramental Community* (London: Darton, Longman & Todd, 1984), p. 35.

[43] Rowan Williams, interviewed as chair of Christian Aid in the Cambridge Alumni magazine Cam 2019/20.

[44] K. Rahner, *Grace in Freedom* (London: Burns and Oates, 1968), pp. 74–5.

[45] At the time of writing, Extinction Rebellion's protest actions are likely to be severely curtailed, if not prohibited, by impending government legislation.

46 The so-called Beatitudes in the New Testament occur in two quite different versions (Luke 6:20–3; Matthew 5:3–12).
47 Pannenberg, *Christian Spirituality*, p. 48.
48 Tobias Winright (ed.), *Green Discipleship: Catholic Theological Ethics and the Environment* (Winona, MN: Anselm Academic, 2011), Chapter 4, "Creation and the Environment in the Hebrew Scriptures", pp. 87–90.